Start Seeing Diversity

The Basic Guide to an Anti-Bias Classroom

by Ellen Wolpert
for the Committee for
Boston Public Housing

Redleaf Press
St. Paul, Minnesota
www.redleafpress.org

Published by Redleaf Press
a division of Resources for Child Caring
10 Yorkton Court
St. Paul, MN 55117
Visit us online at www.redleafpress.org

Redleaf Press books are available at a special discount when purchased in bulk for special premiums and sales promotions. For details, contact the sales manager at 800-423-8309.

Library of Congress Cataloging-in-Publication Data

Wolpert, Ellen.
  Start seeing diversity : the basic guide to an anti-bias classroom / by Ellen Wolpert for the Committee for Boston Public Housing.
     p. cm.
  ISBN-10 : 1-929610-65-3 (pbk.)
  ISBN-13 : 978-1-929610-65-5
  1. Multicultural education. 2. Discrimination—Prevention. 3. Education, Preschool—Curricula. I. Committee for Boston Public Housing. II. Title.
  LC1099.W65 2005
  370.117—dc22

                      2004030693

Manufactured in the United States of America
12 11 10 09 08 07 06 05   8 7 6 5 4 3 2 1

For all of those whose footsteps we follow, who persevere today, and who will continue after in the struggle for social justice.

Contents

Acknowledgments

Special acknowledgment and thanks for the creation of the video must go to all of the staff, children, and families at the Washington-Beech Community Preschool (WBCP). They have participated since April 1986 in the ever-evolving learning process of developing, implementing, reevaluating, and transforming a culturally relevant anti-bias environment.

Special acknowledgment and many thanks must also go to the advisory committee that has been so central to the shaping and reshaping of the slide show, which became the video: Betty Allen, Patti DeRosa, Sheli Wortis, Patty Hnatiuk, Angela Paige-Cook, Margaret Sopin, Mark Murphy, and Richard Ward. Helen McCroskey, Carol Olafajo, and Nancy Dukes played very special roles on the advisory committee, bringing their years of experience with the day-to-day implementation of and reflection on this work at WBCP. Special acknowledgment must also go to Louise Derman-Sparks, whose work, consultation, advice, and mentoring have been invaluable. Our first visit with Louise was like taking a camera that was slightly out of focus and just shifting the lens enough to produce a sharper, crisper image.

Special acknowledgment and thanks also to Bob Sinrod, who was the production consultant for the slide show predecessor of this video.

Special thanks must go to the many colleagues and workshop participants who have viewed the slide show and given their feedback and especially to Lynne Hall, Anna Wexler, Honey Schnapp, Holly Hatch, and many others who provided support and shared their insights and new perspectives.

Portions of the work in the video and in this guide have been specifically adapted from the work of others. The four goals for implementing an anti-bias approach that appear in the introduction of the video and in this guide are adapted from *Anti-Bias Curriculum: Tools for*

Empowering Young Children, by Louise Derman-Sparks and the A.B.C. Task Force (1989), as is the checklist of common stereotypes and biases associated with elderly people. Most other lists of common stereotypes that appear in the guide are adapted from *Guidelines for Selecting Bias-Free Textbooks and Storybooks* from the Council on Interracial Books for Children. The checklist on age is adapted from "Children's Books about the Elderly" by Pat Rigg, Francis E. Kazemek, and Sarah Hudelson (1993). "Responding to Incidents Involving Bias" is adapted from the work of Jane Vella (1994) and the work of Margie Carter and Deb Curtis (1994).

Introduction

The Washington-Beech Community Preschool is located in a public housing development in Boston, Massachusetts. The preschool is the result of the organizing efforts of tenants, working with the Committee for Boston Public Housing, to create a responsive child care program. Since opening in April 1986, the preschool has placed a strong priority on the integration of a multicultural approach. With the help of the book *Anti-Bias Curriculum: Tools for Empowering Young Children,* by Louise Derman-Sparks and the A.B.C. Task Force (1989), as well as a visit with Louise, we were off on a journey that would continually sharpen our focus and strengthen our awareness and inclusion of diversity while also addressing bias related to that diversity.

Rather than assuming that inclusion alone creates respect, we recognize the need to actively address stereotypes and prejudices that preschoolers and adults around them experience and incorporate into their thinking and behavior. Without this proactive approach, children and adults can interact with a variety of people and images yet still internalize the negative values that literally surround them. Messages implying that some groups of people are better than others are embedded in movies, television programs, cartoons, advertisements, books, videos, computer programs, food labels, music, and so on, as well as in the comments and behaviors of friends, family, and the people we and our children encounter in the community, at the local supermarket or pharmacy, gas station or playground. Although much of what we encounter is unintended stereotyping or prejudice, it still has a hurtful impact on adults' and children's developing senses of self and other.

Since beginning this journey we have gone through and continue to go through many reevaluations—from big "aha!"s to microcosmic discoveries. We've made multiple mistakes—or, better said, we've encountered multiple "teachable moments" that often merged into "teachable months." We learned that beautifully illustrated books from the "multicultural" sections of catalogs could and do contain and perpetuate stereotypes. We learned that many of the very beautiful, carefully chosen pictures of people from diverse parts of the world that we had so painstakingly mounted on the walls or covered in Con-Tact paper for classroom games weren't necessarily the ones most relevant to our children. We learned that pictures of children in African villages didn't reflect urban African American children and that rural scenes from the Caribbean didn't reflect the urban backgrounds of immigrant families from Port-au-Prince, Haiti.

We learned that multiculturalism is about all of us, that we all belong "at the table" together—it's not about visiting other people and then going back to a table that remains as it was before our travels. We learned that independence is a central cultural value for some, while interdependence is more central to others, that, for example, giving up a pacifier at age four is not the norm, but a norm in some groups. We learned that we could offend each other without meaning to, that our own defensiveness could be a bigger barrier than ignorance, and that the impact of racism is like an iceberg with infinite subtleties below the waterline that we've only begun to fathom.

We learned that the inclusion of all the books, pictures, puzzles, dolls, and other materials in the world does not by itself assure an anti-bias approach. They are but some of the tools to trigger and stimulate the ongoing process: the conversation, the questioning, the search for information, the construction of knowledge and skills to challenge stereotypes, bias, and injustice related to racism, sexism, classism, ageism, ableism, homophobia, and ethnocentrism. We learned, finally, that we have a lot to teach each other and a lot to learn. And the more we do this, the closer we get and the more exhilarating it feels!

Using This Book

This book begins with an explanation of a basic anti-bias approach and eight guiding assumptions in developing that approach. It then devotes a chapter to each major area of bias; each chapter includes information on stereotypes and truths, scenarios, and discussion questions. Finally, the appendices include guidelines for group facilitators, a checklist for creating and assessing anti-bias environments, a guide to analyzing children's books, the directions for making photograph games like the ones used at Washington-Beech, guidelines for challenging racism and other oppression, and guidelines for responding to incidents involving bias.

The chapters on biases and their accompanying discussion questions are designed to provide information as well as encourage readers to look into their own memories and experiences. Also, they are designed to encourage readers to recognize that their own experiences may be limited. Our hope is that, in reading and responding to the information in this book and in hearing the feelings and perspectives of others, people will expand their knowledge and understanding of the extent and impact of bias and inequity in their many forms. These lists are not definitive works on each subject: you may be aware of stereotypes and bias from your experience that have not been included. Making additions and discussing why they are stereotypes or reflections of bias will strengthen everyone's understanding of the issues and ability to contradict those biases when encountered.

About the Book and the Video

The *Start Seeing Diversity* video is an attempt to share what we have learned. While this book can be used alone to help create an anti-bias classroom, we hope you will also choose to view the video. While the video and the book are both helpful tools, they do not provide a recipe—though some of the provided concrete strategies will work for you as they have worked for us, other strategies will need to be adapted to meet the specific needs of your own program. Our cultural styles may be different from yours. Our mix of ethnic, racial, and class backgrounds may be different from yours. Many factors will determine how you adapt an anti-bias approach. The video can be a catalyst for you to think and talk about bias in relation to yourselves and the children and families you serve.

We hope the book and the video will increase the understanding that children are indeed affected by bias and that integrating an anti-bias approach into programs for children is vital. The book and video show in concrete ways that this is possible, and they also provide practical suggestions you can actually adapt and use.

Like the *Start Seeing Diversity* video, the book has eight sections. First there is a brief summary of the four goals of an anti-bias approach. Then we discuss some of the underlying assumptions that shape the way we use the four goals in our program. This is followed by sections on six areas of bias: age, gender, sexual orientation, economic class, physical abilities and characteristics, and race and ethnicity. In the book and the video, these sections provide many concrete examples from the children, families, and staff in our program. Each also discusses the ways we have responded, as well as other strategies for developing respect for diversity, ways to involve family members in developing a culturally relevant anti-bias approach, and some of the challenges we have experienced and channeled into insight and changes in practice.

We developed the chapters in this book and the sections of the video on each bias in order to provide an introduction to an anti-bias approach and a catalyst to examine in more depth at least some of the biases that affect all of us, as well as to help translate that growing awareness into program strategies and classroom curriculum.

We hope the information provided in this book as well as the video is important and helpful. But to do this work effectively, continual efforts to understand how it all works—reading, forming discussion groups, and going to available trainings or conferences—are essential.

General Discussion Questions for Chapters on Biases

1. What in this chapter was particularly meaningful for you?

2. What do you have questions or disagreements about?

3. Were any issues addressed in the chapter that you feel are inappropriate for young children?

4. Was anything addressed that you feel is appropriate but you feel uncomfortable addressing with young children? with adults?

5. What childhood memories do you have, in or out of school, of learning about or being exposed to stereotypes and bias related to this topic? Are there additions you would make based on your experience?

   • Describe the sources or situations of these memories.

   • Did anyone intervene then?

   • What do you think could have been done?

6. In what ways have you noticed these stereotypes reflected in your nonwork environment? in your work environment? Consider books, movies, television, newspapers, radio, greeting cards, music, advertising (including billboards as well as television commercials, magazine advertisements, and other sources), store displays, and clothing. Are you aware of individuals or groups who have challenged any of these stereotypes?

7. Does this chapter raise or respond to issues in ways that require adaptation or change to be relevant to the cultural practices of the families and staff in your program? For example, using direct forms of communication with people who use

more indirect forms, or stressing individual feelings, needs, or solutions with people who are accustomed to stressing group needs.

8. Have differences in cultural expectations related to issues in this chapter come up or caused conflict in your program?

- Have they been addressed? If not, why not? If yes, how?

- How have you expressed your own or the school's view while respecting cultural differences that you think reflect bias?

9. Is there anything you would like to implement but are not sure how?

10. Are there other behaviors or policies related to this chapter that you have questions about or would like help figuring out?

11. Do you have concerns about others' responses to issues related to this chapter that might make implementation difficult in your setting?

Chapter 1

The Four Goals
for an Anti-Bias Approach

The four goals for an anti-bias approach are for children across all age groups. They are also for the adults who raise and teach children. To effectively implement an anti-bias approach that cultivates the four goals in children's development, we need to cultivate them in our own development as well. We must constantly increase understanding of our own identity, our skills for interacting with diversity, our ability to recognize bias and injustice, and our willingness to act against it. For these reasons many of the discussion questions are designed to help adults reflect on our own identity development and experiences with bias. These discussions will help provide insight into what our own experiences have taught us. They will help us add on to that learning and translate it into effective ways to work with children.

The ways people work toward the four goals must take into account diverse developmental levels as well as our own diverse cultural styles and those of the children and adults with whom we are working. While the goals may be the same for all of us, the specific strategies will vary from person to person and from program to program. A central challenge is to continually develop our awareness of how children and adults communicate and learn and of what cultural factors influence them in doing so. We must also commit ourselves to deepening our understanding of our own cultural lenses, how they differ from or are similar to the lenses of others, and what the implications of the differences are for effective communication and facilitation of learning. For example, in addressing Goal 4, if we want children to develop strategies for challenging bias, and our style is to be direct about an issue but the culture of the child and their family is to be indirect, we will face the challenge of navigating or negotiating between cultural differences. This requires an awareness of diverse styles and the creative willingness to explore, develop, and support a variety of strategies.

Goal 1

Nurture the construction of a knowledgeable, confident identity as an individual and as a member of multiple cultural groups (such as gender, race, ethnicity, or class).

This means creating the educational conditions in which all children are able to like who they are without needing to feel superior to anyone else.

The negative bias many of us learn and begin to believe about ourselves is often called "internalized oppression." We can also internalize messages of superiority if the majority of messages about a group we belong to are positive while those about other groups are negative.

Goal 1 also means enabling children who are not of the dominant culture to develop the ability to operate within both their home culture and the dominant culture, and to negotiate and problem solve when issues arise from differences between the two.

Discussion Questions

- How did you construct a knowledgeable and confident self-identity (in relation to your gender, race, ethnicity, or class)? Did your educational experience nurture the process?

- What are some of the messages of *inferiority* you internalize when the majority of messages about a group you belong to are *negative* while those about other groups are positive?

- What are some of the messages of *superiority* you internalize when the majority of messages about a group you belong to are *positive* while those about other groups are negative?

- Describe a time when you were in a setting dominated by cultural values that were unfamiliar or different from your own. How did that feel? What difficulties did you experience?

- What are some of the challenges or difficulties faced by members of subordinate cultural groups learning to operate in both their own and the dominant culture?

- What are some of the challenges or difficulties faced by members of a dominant cultural group learning to operate in ways that include or are sensitive to cultures of relevant subordinate cultural groups?

Goal 2

Promote comfortable, empathic interaction with people from diverse backgrounds.

This means guiding children's developing awareness of difference in a way that fosters interest in and empathy with difference, rather than a fear or judgment of it. It means helping them develop their skills to negotiate the day-to-day natural discomfort, tensions, problems, or conflicts that can arise from difference. Goal 2 means guiding *all* children—those in the subordinate groups *and* those in dominant groups—to adapt to difference. And it means guiding children to recognize and respect difference while simultaneously recognizing the commonalties all people share.

Discussion Questions

- What were the first messages you learned about differences in general? Where did those messages come from? Were they positive? negative? mixed?

- What were the first messages you learned about differences among people? Where did those messages come from? What values were attached to what differences?

- Recall ways in which you were different from classmates or friends. How did that feel? What messages did you receive?

- Recall ways in which a teacher or other adult helped you, classmates, or friends learn about and deal respectfully with differences. What messages did you receive?

- When someone suggests that a problem exists because there are differences between the two of you, does this raise anxiety? What about the belief that differences are common and generally can be negotiated?

- A Puerto Rican child comes to school with a pacifier. The teachers feel that the child, at age four, is too old to have a pacifier and tell her to leave it in her cubby. Why do you think the teachers responded this way? How might the teachers ask the family about their views on the subject? What do you think the teachers should do if the family says they feel that children should have a pacifier until they no longer want it? (Consider the assumption of superiority—the unexamined idea that one's own ways are natural or right.)

Goal 3

Foster each child's ability to recognize bias and injustice.

This means creating conditions for children to develop the knowledge and analytical skills to identify unfair and untrue images (stereotypes), comments (teasing, name-calling), and behaviors (discrimination) directed at one's own or another's identity. It means knowing that bias hurts.

Discussion Questions

- Recall an early memory of an image, comment, or behavior directed at *your identity* that was untrue or unfair. Describe how you came to realize it was an unfair or untrue stereotype, prejudice, or form of discrimination. How did this realization feel?

- Recall an early memory of an image, comment, or behavior directed at *someone else's identity* that was untrue or unfair. Describe how you came to realize it was an unfair or untrue stereotype, prejudice, or form of discrimination.

- Recall a time when you resisted attempts to help you recognize an untrue or unfair stereotype, prejudice, or form of discrimination. Why did you resist taking in this information?

- Recall when others resisted your attempts to help them recognize something as an untrue or unfair stereotype, prejudice, or form of discrimination. Why do you think there was resistance to the information you were trying to communicate?

Goal 4

Cultivate each child's ability to stand up, individually and with others, against bias or injustice.

This means helping every child learn and practice a variety of ways to act in the face of bias expressed by other children and adults.

Discussion Questions

- What messages do you remember receiving as a child about standing up against things that are unfair? What messages do you hear in your environment now?

- Tell a story for each of the following scenarios. After each story, consider these questions: How did you feel after the incident? How would you have liked to handle the situation?

  —Tell a story about a time when you were a child and someone either did or did not stand up for you against something that was unfair or unjust. Tell another story about this subject from adulthood.

  —Tell a story about a time when you were a child and you either did or did not stand up for someone else against something that was unfair or unjust. Tell another story about this subject from adulthood.

Discussing the Goals

In any discussion of the goals, it's important to emphasize the need to address *all four goals* as we begin our own journeys of awareness and develop implementation strategies. Many people focus primarily on Goal 2 and inadvertently fail to address Goals 1, 3, and 4. Goal 1 is often omitted if there's an assumption that anti-bias work is primarily about relating to others (Goal 2). In fact, Goal 2 requires Goal 1's development of a knowledgeable, confident self-identity and group identity. Often Goals 3 and 4 are left out as people include diversity but do not also foster each child's critical thinking about bias or cultivate each child's ability to stand up, individually and with others, in the face of it.

General Discussion Questions

- What do each of the four goals mean to you?

- Do these goals reflect what you thought a culturally relevant anti-bias approach was about?

- Do any of the goals raise questions or concerns for you?

- What memories do you have of learning to identify bias against your own group or against another group?

- What experiences do you have, as an individual or in a group, of standing up against bias and injustice?

Chapter 2

Eight Guiding Assumptions

The anti-bias work we do with children and adults is guided by a set of assumptions. The assumptions provide a general framework for broadly identifying why we do this work, with whom, and how. The later sections on each area of bias provide more specific strategies. Spending some time identifying these assumptions and discussing them and their implications helps to address some of the most commonly expressed general concerns about this work. The eight assumptions are also covered in the introduction to the *Start Seeing Diversity* video.

Discussing the Eight Assumptions

Below is information about each assumption, examples and scenarios illustrating each, and questions. You can use the scenarios and examples to role-play the assumptions.

If you have the *Start Seeing Diversity* video, read through the definitions of each guiding assumption before seeing the video's introduction. After watching the introduction, take a few minutes to write down any thoughts stimulated by viewing it. Here are some general discussion questions that cover all eight assumptions; specific questions and scenarios also follow each assumption.

General Discussion Questions

1. Do any of the guiding assumptions have particular meaning for you?

2. Are any of them particularly helpful? Can you talk about why?

3. Do any of the guiding assumptions raise questions or disagreement? Which ones? Why?

Assumption 1

Even very young children notice differences and begin to discriminate based on them.

While many adults assume that children don't notice or discriminate based on the differences they see, our own observations and experience tell us they do. As children try to figure out the world around them, they notice obvious physical differences. They also notice the disparity between how things "should be" and how things "really are." They ask questions about the differences and act based on the answers they receive. They need help figuring out the contradictions they encounter.

Research can shed light on children's awareness and thinking that may not be so easily detected by our own observations. Some good examples of interactions that reflect children's awareness of differences and related bias that are hidden from casual observation can be found in "Reframing Classroom Research: A Lesson from the Private World of Children" by A. Alton-Lee, G. Nuthall, and J. Patrick (1993).

The following examples also demonstrate some of the differences that young children have seen and responded to in our program:

- A child picks up a broom handle, uses it as a cane, and says, "Now I'm an old man." He has absorbed societal messages about how old people are different from younger people.

- Children are jumping rope, and one child declares, "Boys can jump higher than girls!" Another boy comments to his play partner, "You can't be the doctor cuz you're a girl."

- A child says, "You can't have two mommies."

- Looking at a photograph of a woman in a wheelchair bathing a baby, a child says, "People in wheelchairs can't be mommies."

- A child identifies a picture of an unknown black man saying, "He's a robber cuz he has a brown face like a robber."

- A child says, "They're not real Indians. Real Indians wear feathers."

- A child sees a photo of a baby being carried in a basket and says, "Babies don't go in baskets!"

- Can you think of other comments you have heard children make that indicate their awareness of differences—concrete physical differences as well as more subtle differences they have begun to believe exist between various groups of people?

- How would you respond to the following scenario? Someone you work with says, "Young children don't notice differences. If we point them out, we'll just be making trouble unnecessarily."

Assumption 2

It's not a problem that children notice differences. The problem is that in our society, some differences are valued as positive and others as negative, and children absorb and act on these values.

Differences exist. Pretending we don't notice them does not make them go away. The problem is when we place values on those differences and then act or react based on those values. Pretending we don't notice differences stops us from analyzing how those differences affect our lives—how they offer advantages to some people and disadvantages to others. In what ways are these advantages and disadvantages fair or unfair? What can we do to change these conditions? Not acknowledging our differences stops us from being able to negotiate conflicts that arise because of them.

For example, a child who sees a homeless man and says, "That man's a bum," has already learned to value people who have homes over people who do not. When we define the problem as the child's noticing the difference (some people have homes and some sleep on park benches), it stops us from even asking questions like these:

- Is the problem that the child has noticed the difference that some people have a home(s) and some people are homeless? Or is the problem that we devalue homelessness?

- Why are people homeless? Does joblessness cause homelessness? Can a person with a job be homeless? Does laziness cause homelessness? Can a person who is not lazy be homeless?

- Can you think of reasons for homelessness that do not blame the person who is homeless? (For example, lack of affordable housing or lack of mental health services.)

- Does having the money to live in a home make one a good person?

- A four-year-old boys tells an African American student teacher, "You belong in jail." She asks, "Why?" He replies, "Cuz you're brown."

- A child says, "Ooh, he's fat! I wouldn't be friends with a fat person!"

What differences have these children noticed? What values have they expressed? Is the problem noticing the difference or assigning the value?

Assumption 3

We do not all experience bias in the same way.

Depending on who we are, some of the biases support our identity and some attack it. As mentioned earlier, the negative bias we learn and begin to believe about ourselves is often called internalized oppression. We can also internalize messages of superiority if the majority of messages about a group we belong to are positive while those about other groups are negative. When the biases support our identities, we often develop, without even realizing it, a feeling that our own knowledge, values, and ways of doing things are better than those of others.

Remember that while all children are affected by bias, all children are not affected in the same way. Watch out for attempts to equalize racial oppression. While people of color may hold and express bias against white people, the impact of such bias is not comparable to the level of institutionalized bias (racism) that affects people of color. Such bias can and should be challenged, but it isn't the same as the lived experience of multiple daily microcosmic acts of racism. Nor is it the same as the impact on entire groups of people who are denied justice, employment, housing, decent education and health care, or proportionate and realistic representation in all forms of media.

1. Discuss the following scenarios:

   - You and a friend both attend the same elementary school. Early tests indicate that you both have a high level of intelligence. Your family moves, and you attend a school that is well funded and has extensive resources. As a result, you do well on a very important college entrance exam. Your friend has attended a school that is poorly funded with very few resources. She does badly on the same exam. Are you, therefore, smarter than your friend?

- You graduate from college and go on to get a high-paying job. Your friend, who didn't do well on the test and so could not go to college, is now ineligible for the job you just got hired for. Are you, therefore, superior to your friend? What messages will you receive that suggest your success is based on superiority rather than on opportunity?

- Someone says to you, "I don't understand why we mostly focus on just one side of each issue. We address bias about the poor, but there's bias about the rich too. Why don't we talk as much about that? There's bias about people of color, but also about white people. And there's bias about women and girls, but also about men and boys. Why don't we spend just as much time on that?" How would you respond?

2. Of the following paired groups of people, which one in each pair is primarily advantaged by bias, and which one is primarily disadvantaged by it? (There are always exceptions, but consider overall trends of advantage and disadvantage in the United States: infant mortality, employment rates, income, high school graduation rates, and life expectancy, as well as how groups are reported in the media.)

- Elderly people/Young people

- Males/Females

- Heterosexuals/Homosexuals

- Caucasians/People of color

- Christians/Jews, Muslims, atheists, and so on

- Able-bodied people/People with disabilities

- Rich people/Poor and working-class people

Are there other paired groups you wish to add? Indicate which group in the pair receives the primary advantage and which receives the primary disadvantage.

Most of us receive some advantages and some disadvantages because of our group membership. From the pairs above, make a list of the advantaged groups you are a member of and a list of the disadvantaged groups you are a member of. Are there others you would add to either category?

Assumption 4

An anti-bias approach is important for everyone.

We are all bombarded by bias and stereotypes, both about ourselves and others. We develop biased ideas about people we interact with every day. We also develop biased ideas about people we never meet.

All people are affected by the bias in our society, and we all need to learn critical-thinking skills to deal with it. Anti-bias work is important in programs that are all or mostly white, all or mostly people of color, and racially mixed.

It's important to implement an anti-bias approach in all white groups. Some people argue that an anti-bias approach is not for white children. But white children, like children of color, are bombarded by all the biases in the environment—including bias about age, economic class, ethnicity, family composition, gender, physical and mental abilities, physical characteristics, race, religion, and sexual orientation—and even if they are in classrooms or communities that are all white, children who are white still develop bias based on color. In addition, children don't need direct interaction with others to develop bias about them. The bias is all around them, in books, movies, television, advertising, and of course what they hear from other children and adults.

The absence of people of color in all-white or mostly white programs is just as much a sign of the divide created by racism as are racial clashes in environments that are multiracial. This division and absence of diversity in one's life supports the belief that one's own way or perspective is the only or best one. Just as the existence of diversity requires purposeful attempts to address bias related to that diversity, so does the absence of diversity require purposeful attempts to broaden one's experience and address relevant bias. With changing demographics and life circumstances, it is better to address diversity issues now, rather than be disadvantaged later by the inability to interact in competent and confident ways with a broader range of people.

It's important as well to implement an anti-bias approach in groups comprised entirely of people of color. Children of color are affected by bias about themselves. They often learn to believe it and then perpetuate it as if it were true (internalized oppression). Children of color need to be able to resist the impact of bias and discrimination. Children of color are also affected by other biases, such as sexism, classism, ableism, or homophobia, and need to learn to recognize and not perpetuate those biases as well.

Finally, it's important to implement an anti-bias approach in groups of children who are racially and ethnically diverse. An anti-bias approach involves dealing with many biases in addition to those associated with race and ethnicity. Children in racially and ethnically diverse groups are bombarded, like everyone else, by biases related to age, gender, class, physical abilities, and religion. So there is much work to do. In addition, many people think that racially and ethnically diverse groups don't need to address racial and ethnic biases because they have so many opportunities to interact—to get to know each other and to break down stereotypes and bias. Having experiences with people different from ourselves, however, does not eliminate the impact of bias in our environment unless a conscious effort is made to recognize and address it. Patti DeRosa, an anti-bias/anti-racist trainer from Boston, often gives gender as an example. She says that men and women are together all the time, but being together by itself has done little to eradicate sexism. Unfortunately, the opportunity for playing and working together is not enough. There must be activities and interventions that help children recognize and purposefully challenge the bias they develop about themselves and others.

For example, adults and children all over this country who have never met a Native American have all kinds of ideas about what Native people are like. Here are some examples:

- From many television movies and cartoons, Geoff thought Native people lived only in the past. From leaflets passed out at a Cleveland Indians game, he learned that not only do Native people exist today, they are actively protesting against current stereotypes like the logo and name of the team Geoff had come to see play.

- Shelinda learned in first grade that Columbus discovered America. Later she learned from reading Howard Zinn's *A People's History of the United States* (1997) that there were millions of people in this land living in sophisticated societies when Columbus arrived here, so someone must have discovered this land a long time before him.

- Hugo thought everyone in his community celebrates Thanksgiving because the schools always close for this holiday and his friends celebrate it. When Hugo started a new job, he heard from coworkers that they do not celebrate Thanksgiving, but instead were going to a ceremony mourning the death of Native people and cultures.

1. Role-play the following situation and ask for possible responses: A colleague says to you, "I don't understand why we have to take on this anti-bias stuff. Our kids are all white—they don't need this."

2. If you work in all-white groups or groups that are all children of color, make a list of your concerns about an anti-bias approach. Take a few minutes to brainstorm about each one.

3. Read the scenarios below and discuss them and your reactions to them using the questions that follow:

   • A white child was playing with a puzzle. A second white child wanted to play, too, but the first child preferred to play alone. The second child, in frustration, said, "Well, I don't care. You're just poor white trash anyway!" The teacher was so stunned she blurted out, "I can't believe you said that! That's not okay! Who did you hear that from?!?"

   • While building in the block area, Shanielle and Kelsey, two African American girls, had a disagreement about where to put the blocks. Unable to get her way, Shanielle said angrily to Kelsey, "Well, I don't like you anyway. You've got bad hair. My hair is good."

   • Miriam, who is African American, approached the teacher and said, "Jennifer says I can't play cuz my skin is dirty."

   a. What happened? What bias was being expressed? Why did it happen?

   b. What's the impact of what happened on the children involved and on the classroom in general?

   c. How could you intervene with the children? How would you follow up?

Do you have additional ideas, experiences, or examples of scenarios/incidents/comments from your setting that indicate a need for an anti-bias approach in programs that are all or mostly white, all or mostly children of color, or racially and ethnically mixed?

Assumption 5

As adults, we are often unaware of our biases. Therefore we unintentionally perpetuate the biases in environments we create.

If three-, four-, and five-year-old children have already absorbed stereotypical ideas—that dark-skinned people are robbers, that Native people wear feathers, that fat people are inappropriate as friends, that girls can't jump as high as boys—think of how many other stereotypes and biases we have absorbed in the course of twenty, thirty, forty, or more years of uninterrupted or relatively unchallenged messages from popular culture, advertising, news commentary and visual images, and comments of colleagues, friends, and relatives. Learning these biases and stereotypes is not our fault. Biases that are learned can be unlearned.

If from the beginning we are rarely taught to question or critique but rather to receive and accept information, if the questions we are asked are predominantly those that have correct answers determined by someone else, and if the ways of our families are the dominant ways of thinking and doing things that are constantly being reflected back at us, why would we even consider that there might be other ways, other points of view, or other analyses of why things happen?

In most cases, we have not been trained or encouraged to consider that there might be alternative views as valid as our own or that the information we have received may be biased or even untrue. Ferai Chedaya gives this example of how biased information in the media affects our understanding: Statistically, it is known that the same percentage of people of color and white people uses drugs. However, the images we most often get from the media are people of color using drugs. Large inner-city news agencies in search of visual images to illustrate their stories are usually closer to the predominantly black street drug users than to the predominantly white suburban in-home drug users. Not taught to question, and without many easily available alternative messages, we develop the mistaken idea that drugs are a black problem. We may then make faulty assumptions about the experiences of children in our care or the families they come from.

Changing this, of course, requires some detective work—learning to question and to construct our own knowledge, developing critical thinking skills, uncovering biased or untrue messages, and creating environments that challenge rather than perpetuate them. We can give our students the tools to maintain that process on a lifelong basis as we construct those tools for ourselves.

Sometimes when we have been told that something is biased, we are unable to accept the impact of our actions because we have good intentions and don't mean to perpetuate bias. It's often difficult to acknowledge that there can be a big difference between what we intend and the actual impact of what we do. Many of us base our self-image in wanting to be nonsexist, nonclassist, nonracist—even anti-racist. It's hard to discover that our actions may actually be the opposite of what we want so much for them to be.

I remember a time that an African American colleague had seen a showing of the *Start Seeing Diversity* video in the earlier slide show version. She told me that she thought some parts of it were racist. I kept pestering her to sit down with me and show me these parts so I could change them. She was very hesitant, but finally agreed to review a small segment of the slide show with me. I, of course, considered myself to be extremely open-minded and anti-racist. She began pointing out the parts she perceived as racist, and I proceeded to argue with absolutely everything she had to say. I don't know if her hesitancy to sit down with me was from fear that I would respond this way, but I certainly know now (after hearing from others) that the fear we as whites will defend and argue—rather than listen and understand—often plays a big role in people's unwillingness to provide these insights.

Discussion Questions and Scenarios

Discuss the scenario below and your reaction to it using the questions that follow:

- Jack was wearing a Cleveland Indians t-shirt with the exaggerated, bright red, hook-nosed profile that is the team's logo. Many people protest naming sports teams and using logos in ways that demean Native people by portraying them as distorted cartoon figures. When asked about the shirt, Jack said he was an unbiased person and was wearing the shirt to support the team. He said it was okay to wear the shirt even though some people found it offensive because he didn't mean it that way. His intent was positive. The impact was negative.

1. What do you think about Jack's reaction that it's okay to do something that offends someone else as long as your intent is not to offend? What would you say to him?

2. Think of a time you tried to tell someone that a well-intentioned act or comment was actually offensive. Did you encounter the defensive insistence "But I didn't mean it that way"? Why do you think the person responded that way? Do you think something could have been done differently to reduce their defensiveness and increase their willingness to listen and try to understand?

3. Think of a time when someone tried to tell you that the content of something you did or said was offensive and you defensively insisted, "I didn't mean it that way." What were you feeling? What would have made it easier to listen and try to fully understand the feedback rather than be defensive?

Assumption 6

Understanding bias and inequality is a long-term process that can be difficult as well as exhilarating and fun.

The process of unlearning old ways and developing new ones requires a long-term commitment to critical inquiry and self-reflection. Rather than a single workshop or course, it is a lifelong process of both exhilarating discoveries and barely noticeable shifts. It takes time to learn to see the roles we each play within systems of advantages and disadvantages, to reevaluate our accumulated miseducation, to learn to critically reexamine what we have held true for so long, and to transfer a new awareness into the classroom.

One of the difficulties I have encountered is that, after a single workshop or course, some people feel they've learned what they need to know. For some this idea of "long term" may seem discouraging. For others it is a new lens and set of tools with which to analyze and attempt to solve the day-to-day and ongoing challenges inherent in working with people. For some it is a relief to realize that one cannot be expected to know everything. We all will make mistakes and more mistakes, come to new awareness and change practices we were once proud of, and then sometimes change them again.

I have found exhilaration in the ability to see things I couldn't see before and to understand the perspectives that in an unintentionally arrogant way I once found so easy to reject. For example, several years ago an African American colleague who grew up in the southern United States was describing her experience with school integration. I'd grown up in the northeastern United States and thought that integration of the schools was the best thing since sliced bread. My colleague described how much she had hated the change from an all-black school where she felt validated to an all-white school where she felt invalidated. As she talked, I sat there wisely nodding my head in visible support and agreement while internally saying to myself, "What's wrong with her?" Not long after that conversation, I read a work by Lisa Delpit in which she described other African Americans' reactions to school integration that were similar to my colleague's. At that point I realized how quick I had been to elevate my own perspective above that of my colleague. Every time this happens it's like having previously closed windows and doors fly open.

Discussion Questions and Scenarios

1. Discuss the scenarios below using the questions that follow them:

   - A teacher was making a serious attempt to create an environment that would be supportive of all the children in the classroom. In an attempt to reflect images relevant to African American children, all the pictures that included black people were those of daily activities in rural African villages. The staff discussed the images, and it became clear that African American children were not likely to see themselves reflected in those pictures. They also reflected the stereotype that Africa has no cities. The teacher, in her growing awareness of bias, was trying to correct a problem—the absence of images reflecting African American children—but in the process uncovered new stereotypes. Slowly her picture collections changed to more effectively portray diversity in nonstereotypical and relevant ways.

- You want to arrange for training in developing an anti-bias approach. A colleague responds by saying, "We already had our workshop on anti-bias for this year." How would you respond?

2. Discuss the following questions:

- Do you have examples of learning related to bias that has taken place over time—practices you once thought to be effective but now recognize as perpetuating bias?

- Do you have questions about current practices or things that you have been considering but are worried may perpetuate bias?

Assumption 7

It's important to create an environment for adults as well as children where everyone's participation is sought after and valued and where it's okay to disagree.

Part of building trust is developing strategies that effectively include and value everyone's participation. Including some people is easy—you ask them to join in and they do. With others it's not that simple. Some people are not convinced that their opinions matter—it's one of the barriers that their experiences of bias have created. These people need to know that their serious reflection and willingness to talk about what they are feeling and why will be treated with serious respect. For many, diverse cultural expectations can make participation difficult. Seeking everyone's participation requires serious reflection on the effects of bias as well as on diverse cultural patterns of participation, respect, dealing with disagreement, and so forth.

Some people aren't able to play strong roles in group dynamics until it has been proven to them that people in positions of power are committed to sharing some of that power. Sometimes this commitment requires paying serious attention to the silences as well as to what is said aloud. Insights from reading and watching videos can help in understanding many of the dynamics of racism, sexism, classism, and ethnocentrism. Here are some helpful resources in addressing this issue:

Black and White Styles in Conflict, by Thomas Kochman. 1995. Chicago: University of Chicago Press.

Color of Fear video, by Lee Mun Wah. n.d. Berkeley: Stir Fry Productions.

Diversity, Independence, and Individuality; Diversity: Contrasting Perspectives; Diversity and Communication; and *Diversity and Conflict Management,* a four-video series. n.d. Crystal Lake, IL: Magna Systems.

Talking 9 to 5: Women and Men at Work, by Deborah Tannen. 2001. New York: Quill.

In many cases people who are male, white, college educated, or native English speakers unintentionally set the tone of or dominate the discussion, or determine which subjects are covered, by being the first to speak, speaking the longest or most frequently, or having the last word. To overcome this tendency, it may be necessary to structure the discussion in ways that prevent these patterns from being established: for example, by ensuring that a person of color speaks first or that a woman speaks after each man.

Developing trust requires recognizing and validating diverse cultural and personal styles of communication and conflict. Often we ascribe conflict to personal characteristics we can't do anything about. Instead we need to learn about cultural and personal style differences and identify the differences that exist in our settings. Openly acknowledging that such differences exist and that they are a natural part of human interaction makes it possible to agree on strategies that can reduce some of the resulting difficulties or conflicts.

Discussion Questions and Scenarios

Using the questions below, discuss this challenge of creating an environment that supports everyone's participation:

1. What factors or styles create trust for you in a work setting?

2. Describe your communication style. What aspects of the styles of others make you uncomfortable, or create anxiety, tension, or dislike?

3. What makes a good argument? Is there such a thing? What makes you comfortable or uncomfortable in an argument?

4. Can you identify communication style differences that exist in your setting? What impact do they have? What strategies might you consider in dealing with these differences?

Assumption 8

It's important to integrate an anti-bias approach into all parts of the program.

Much of what children learn comes not from the planned or acknowledged curriculum but from the "hidden curriculum"—all the interactions and unplanned messages that go on along with and inside the lessons. For this reason, an anti-bias approach must be a way of thinking that is part of an entire program's environment, including policies, written materials, and curriculum. It's reflected in the interactions among children, among adults, and between adults and children. An anti-bias approach is not an "add-on."

Adults often worry that if they raise issues of bias that children haven't specifically expressed, children will learn about something bad unnecessarily. In fact young children are bombarded by stereotypes and biased attitudes. These messages will affect their self-images, attitudes, and behavior toward others unless consistent efforts are made to provide the children with the critical-thinking skills and self-confidence necessary to question and reject the negative messages. We would like to believe in the "innocence of childhood," but we cannot be naive about the realities that surround children. For some that means the direct experience of poverty, racism, and other forms of discrimination. For others it may come from indirect experience in the form of popular television cartoons and movies.

Consider the following scenarios and discuss them using the questions that follow:

• You are in a staff meeting and one of your coworkers says, "I think an anti-bias curriculum will make things worse. If you point out differences, children will start seeing differences they didn't know were there. If you talk about stereotypes, you will be teaching things they wouldn't otherwise learn. Besides, it's better to emphasize the positive—how we're alike—rather than the negative—how we're different."

• In a staff meeting someone says, "But children shouldn't be exposed to unpleasant biases. Childhood should be a time of innocence and protection from these things. Children shouldn't have to deal with ableism, sexism, racism, poverty, or homelessness. These are inappropriate subjects for early childhood classrooms."

What is happening in each scenario? What might the legitimate concerns of the speaker be? How might you respond?

Not all children will be able to articulate the bias in their environment. For those who are able to, we can implement strategies to elicit their ideas and then develop responsive curriculum. For children too young to articulate such complex ideas, it is important that we monitor major influences on them, provide alternative messages, and model questions and other strategies that lay a foundation for critical thinking.

For example, in the movie *The Lion King*, the villainous Scarface has a black mane, and the hyenas who destroy Pride Rock are dark in color. The heroes, on the other hand, are golden. Among the bad hyenas who move in and destroy "the neighborhood" is the only voice using a distinctly African American form of speech. I know of a five-year-old child who left the movie and said, "Black people are bad." If we explicitly examine the use of the color black, we are less likely to allow it to slide into subconscious awareness. The bias can be noticed and rejected. In responding to *The Lion King*'s effect on children's thinking we can collect pictures of black people doing diverse activities and talk about them with children, asking about their feelings and perceptions. We can create games with lots of positive images and ask children to describe the images as they play, including skin color. We can make comparisons between these images and those in the movie. What characters in the movie have any black on them? Do any of the "good" animals have black clothes or black skin or black hair? Do you think it's fair that most of the bad animals are black or wear black or have a part of them that is black?

In thinking about implementing an anti-bias approach, people often worry about learning new strategies, planning new activities, and then adding on to what they already do. An anti-bias approach can often be implemented, however, by adapting familiar strategies and activities—shifting the lens, changing the focus.

Discussion Questions and Scenarios

Discuss the scenario below using the questions that follow it:

- Two children are working together on a computer using a program to enhance math skills. A picture of a hippopotamus comes up on the screen. One of the children says, "Ooh, he's fat! I wouldn't be friends with a fat person!" A teacher and several children working with a number bingo game at a nearby table hear the remark. One of the children at the table is fat. When he hears the remark, he has a visible reaction and puts his head down. The teacher, who is attempting to assess the math skills of each child at the table, ignores the remark and continues the game, concerned that if she stops, some children won't get a turn.

1. What have the children at both the computer and the table learned during this work period?

2. Assisting children to develop thinking skills is an important goal in most classrooms. Asking open-ended questions designed to encourage children to think for themselves is a common strategy. What open-ended questions might you apply to this scenario?

3. Assisting children to develop problem-solving and conflict-resolution skills is an important goal in most classrooms. Creating puppet or persona doll stories about problems children have is a common strategy. What kind of puppet story might you create to follow up on the above scenario?

4. Assisting children to develop literacy skills is also an important goal in most classrooms. Reading, creating, and telling stories are common strategies. What kind of story might you tell or create to follow up on the above scenario? What kind of stories might children be able to create?

Chapter 3

Bias Related to Age

Ageism is any attitude, action, or institutional practice that subordinates people based on their age. While ageism works against both old and young people, young people also benefit from ageism, so this section deals only with discrimination against older people. Distorted representations of old people in books, films, TV, newspapers, and other media lead a majority of us to feel that older people's mental and physical capabilities are inevitably inferior due to their age. An even more serious consequence is that the bias resulting from these depictions keeps many older people in U.S. society severely impoverished, excludes them from satisfying work, and encourages their treatment as useless, unwanted, and unattractive citizens.

Evaluate materials (including books, videos, posters, manipulatives, block play figures), classroom practices, and conversations for these and other age-related stereotypes:

A. General stereotypes about older people:

Older men:	Older women:
hard of hearing	rocking in a chair
walking with a cane	boring
forgetful	old-fashioned
rocking in a chair	frumpy clothing
blank-faced	stubborn
bent body	asexual
wearing baggy clothes	knitting all day

asexual	ugly old shrew
cruel and frightening	wicked witch
all-wise and patient	sad and helpless
	meddling in family affairs

B. Stereotypical story lines associated with age:

- A short idyllic relationship between a child and an older person is interrupted by death.

- An older person is unhappy until a child intervenes and plays or spends time with her.

- An older character has a walk-on role as someone who is frightening, funny, or sad.

- Elderly people are segregated from activities involving people of other ages.

- Elderly people are portrayed as decrepit grandparents.

- Information is often omitted about the particular problems and needs of older people, such as fixed incomes, limitations of poverty, or stigmas based on age.

- Real perspectives of elderly characters are ignored in favor of a point of view of a child observing an elderly person.

- Young people are often portrayed as fearing or disliking people who are elderly.

- Older people are portrayed as having no occupation or useful role.

C. Stereotypic illustrations associated with age:

- Older people are excluded from group scenes when they could logically appear.

- Elderly people are illustrated with stereotypic props, such as canes, bent bodies, sagging clothes, or rocking chairs.

- Older people are illustrated as lacking personality and variety.

D. Stereotypic language and terminology associated with age:

- Dehumanizing or limiting descriptors such as old, little, small, sad, and poor are overused.

- Phrases like "the old woman" or "the old man" are substituted for elderly people's names.

- Derogatory statements such as "You can't teach an old dog new tricks" and "There's no fool like an old fool" are often used.

Use these truths to counteract the stereotypes:

Many older people remain physically and mentally active and have full and interesting lives whether or not they are involved with young children. Most grandparents are in their forties and fifties and are quite active during their grandchildren's early years. Most young children are not afraid of or bored with older people until affected by distorted story lines and other stereotypes.

Many problems faced by older people are caused by societal injustice rather than by the fact of being old. Many older people do work and many more would if not for employer bias, forced retirement, or other forms of discrimination. While it is true that many older people are lonely and unhappy, the reasons are often tied to poverty and isolation because of stigmas related to age, rather than to age itself.

Many older people are active in their communities and happily involved with people of all ages. Many other older people are content in their solitude. Many older people actively learn new things, as the success of Elderhostel programs testifies. Many old people have valuable skills, perspectives, and information to share with younger people.

Sources

Guidelines for selecting bias-free textbooks and storybooks. 1980. New York: Council on Interracial Books for Children.

Rigg, Pat, Francis E. Kazemek, and Sarah Hudelson. Spring 1993. Children's books about the elderly. *Rethinking Schools.*

Discussion Questions and Scenarios

Discuss the following scenarios in terms of what issues they raise related to ageism and what you would do in response:

- You are doing a workshop on ageism using the material in this chapter. You ask what people think about statements such as "You can't teach an old dog new tricks." One of the participants responds, "Well, what about the studies that prove older people can't learn as fast as younger ones?"

- In a meeting of adults, you're looking at photographs of elderly people. One of the photos shows an elderly woman shoveling snow. Someone in your group says, "She's too old to do that!"

- A four-year-old picks up a broom handle, uses it as a cane, and says, "Now I'm an old man."

- You have created a collection of photographs that reflect elderly people as independent and active and engaged in social activities outside the home. Another staff person tells you that the pictures do not represent how elderly people really are and that you should include pictures of elderly people in wheelchairs or sick in bed.

Chapter 4

Bias Related to Gender

S_exism_ is any attitude, action, or institutional practice that subordinates people because of their gender or assigns roles in society based on gender. It is prejudice based on gender that is backed up by institutional power to impose that prejudice in ways that advantage one gender and disadvantage the other. In addition, sexism is reflected in cultural definitions of masculinity and femininity that prevent people of all genders from realizing their full human potential. Although both men and women are damaged by sexism in this way, men also benefit from sexism in terms of social, political, and financial power while women do not. Women are the targets of sexism because they are systematically disadvantaged by this bias in ways that men are not.

Evaluate materials (including books, videos, posters, manipulatives, block play figures), classroom practices, and conversations for these and other gender stereotypes:

A. Gender stereotypes:

Men:	**Women:**
active	passive
brave	frightened
strong	weak
rough	gentle
competitive	gives up easily
intelligent	unoriginal
logical	silly

quiet	illogical
easygoing	always talking
decisive	gossipy
problem solver	shrewish
messy	nagging
tall	easily confused
mechanical	problem solver
independent	neat
leader	short
inventive/innovator	inept
expresses anger	dependent
unemotional	follower
plays or works outdoors	conformer
unconcerned about appearance	controls anger
roughhouses with children	emotional
adventurer	plays or works indoors
leader	concerned about appearance
	nurtures children
	has innate need for marriage and motherhood
	supporter

B. Occupational stereotypes associated with gender:

Females are often placed in, and males excluded from, occupations such as houseparent, nurse, teacher, secretary, librarian, sewer of clothing, maid, flight attendant, and volunteer. At the same time, men are often placed in, and women excluded from, occupations such as firefighting, bus or truck driver, principal, mechanic, carpenter, plumber, lawyer, banker, and doctor.

C. Stereotypical story lines associated with gender:

- Males confront and solve problems more often than females.

- Rite of passage stories. For example, a boy becomes a man through an ordeal or physical trial. These stories make children equate "manhood" with brute strength and promote a macho, militaristic mentality. There are fewer coming-of-age stories for girls, and they rarely involve the same kind of physical trial.

- An absence of cross-gender activities and friendships, suggesting that connections should be made based on gender rather than human qualities.

- Success for girls is often based on an extraordinary feat in order to be accepted by boys. For example, girls have to hit the winning run or in some other way fit into male standards of success.

- Being a "tomboy" is acceptable as long as she eventually becomes a "proper young lady." Young girls are often portrayed as enterprising and active while older women are portrayed in traditional roles, such as housewife and mother.

- Information about sexism and struggle for equality in both a historic and a current context is often excluded, where it would make sense to include it.

D. Stereotypical illustrations related to gender:

- Numerically, there are more images of males than females.

- Male images are often more central in terms of placement and activity.

- Males are most often taller than females.

- Females are often dressed inappropriately for the activity.

- Different art styles and colors are often used for males and females.

- Men and women often lack a full range of emotions.

- Toys are often assigned by gender.

E. Bias in language and terminology associated with gender:

- Male nouns, pronouns, or suffixes are used to represent both genders.
  Example: man-made versus synthetic or manufactured

- Equivalent constructions are not used when presenting people of both genders in similar roles.
  Example: man and wife versus man and woman or husband and wife

- Women's first names are used in places where men's full names or last names are used.
  Example: "Frederick Douglass and Harriet Tubman were great Americans. Douglass was a writer, speaker, and leader, while Harriet bravely . . ." versus "Frederick Douglass and Harriet

Tubman were great Americans. Douglass was a writer, speaker, and leader, while Tubman bravely . . ."

- Words or expressions are used that ascribe certain human traits only to males or females.
  Example: feminine, masculine, "the fairer sex," sissy, hussy, tomboy

- Descriptors or word endings are used to denote a female, suggesting that this role is not usually or normally a woman's.
  Example: actress versus actor; lady coach versus coach

- Females are described in terms of their appearance or relationship to men in ways not used when describing males.
  Example: "Principal Warren Sweet and his attractive assistant, Mary Ayers, wife of football coach Phil Ayers" versus "Principal Warren Sweet and his assistant, Mary Ayers" or "Gray-haired, handsome Principal Warren Sweet and his attractive, blonde assistant, Mary Ayers"

- Language is used to imply that an otherwise gender-neutral phrase refers to men, that men have control over women, or that women are less important than men.
  Example: "The pioneers faced many hardships while bringing their families along the trail" versus "Pioneer families faced many hardships while traveling along the trail."

Use these truths to counteract the stereotypes:

Gender identity is learned through culture rather than being primarily a function of physical gender. If biology were the primary determinant, then we would not be able to find gender role differences existing by ethnic or national culture, as indeed they do. Females and males act differently in different cultures, depending on what has been defined as gender appropriate (in other words, masculine or feminine) in that culture.

World-famous anthropologist Margaret Mead (1969) maintains that gender identity and gender roles are mainly learned rather than innate. She writes: "Many, if not all, of the personality traits which we have called masculine or feminine are as lightly linked to sex as are the clothing, the manners, and the form of headdress that a society at a given period assigns to either sex. . . . The evidence is overwhelmingly in favor of the strength of social conditioning."

1. Change the following to reflect nonsexist language:

brotherhood	man-sized
cameraman	middleman
foreman	repairman
freshman	saleswoman
mailman	poetess
manpower	

Each student must read his book.

A good nurse respects her patients.

John Smith and his wife.

Coaches Wagner and Patty Jones

Sit up and act like a lady.

Be a good girl, Mary.

You think like a man.

Don't cry, Joey. Take it like a man.

Sue Sennis, wife of Dr. John Sennis, and Lew Morgan

Congress finally granted women the vote in 1919.

In many ancient Indian societies men allowed women to control the family and the home.

2. Discuss interactions with children that you have participated in or witnessed, in which children received gender-biased messages like the following:

- Giving boys the impression that their play or work is more important than that of girls by avoiding interrupting boys but more freely interrupting girls to take on a different task or activity

- Encouraging girls to clean up even if they don't want to but avoiding conflict with boys rather than encouraging them to clean up as well

- Defining girls who are watching as participants while defining boys who are watching as watching and actively encouraging them to participate

- Commenting on girls' appearance and on boys' performance

- Encouraging girls to express feelings but distracting boys from feelings

- Encouraging boys to express their opinions, including dis-agreement, while more often encouraging girls to agree at the expense of their own opinions

3. Discuss the following scenarios. How would you respond? What would you do to follow up on the initial discussion?

- Three children are playing "hospital." One of the children is the patient while the other two both want to be the doctor. You overhear a boy say, "You can't be the doctor. You're a girl!"

- A group of children are jumping rope. Teachers are holding the rope. One of the boys jumps in, and when his turn is finished, he announces, "Boys can jump higher than girls!"

- Carol comes to pick up Shola at the preschool. She shares with you a problem she's having. Her son wants a doll. Every day and everywhere they go he talks about how much he wants a doll. But Carol's mother and sister keep telling her that boys who play with dolls become sissies.

Sources

Jenkins, Jeanne Kohl, and Pam MacDonald. 1979. *Growing up equal: Activities and resources for parents and teachers of young children.* Englewood Cliffs, NJ: Prentice Hall.

Leipzig, Judith. 1992. Helping whole children grow: Nonsexist child-rearing for infants and toddlers. In *Alike and different: Exploring our humanity with young children,* edited by Bonnie Neugebauer. Washington, DC: National Association for the Education of Young Children.

Mead, Margaret. 1969. *Sex and temperament in three primitive societies.* New York: Dell Publishing.

Stanford, Beverly Hardcastle. 1996. Gender equity in the classroom. In *Common bonds: Anti-bias teaching in a diverse society,* edited by Deborah A. Byrnes and Gary Kiger. Olney, MD: Association for Childhood Education International.

Chapter 5

Bias Related to Sexual Orientation

Homophobia is the oppression of a group of people because of their sexual orientation as lesbian, gay, or bisexual. (A *lesbian* is a woman who forms her primary loving and sexual relationships with other women. A *gay* man is a man who forms his primary loving and sexual relationships with other men. A *bisexual* person forms primary loving and sexual relationships with members of either sex.) Homophobia is closely connected with sexism and is often used to keep people from moving outside their assigned gender roles for fear of being labeled gay or lesbian.

Homophobia includes social standards and norms that dictate heterosexuality as moral and normal and homosexuality as abnormal and immoral, backed up by institutional power that privileges heterosexual people and denies privilege to gay, lesbian, and bisexual people. It includes the many ways governments, businesses, churches, and other institutions and organizations discriminate against people on the basis of sexual orientation. Examples are stated policies against lesbian, gay, or bisexual people holding office; state laws that disallow local equal rights ordinances; the denial of the financial, legal, and social benefits of civil marriage to lesbian and gay couples; employee benefits that allow heterosexual people to cover spouses and children while refusing that coverage to the partners and children of lesbian and gay employees; and norms that prevent gay, lesbian, and bisexual employees from bringing their same-sex partners to company functions while encouraging heterosexuals to bring theirs.

Homophobia affects children in several ways. First of all, many children are being raised by parents who are gay or lesbian. These children need their families to be supported by the child care or educational environments they are in. Second, as with other biases, children frequently pick up homophobic attitudes ("Only boys can marry girls") and use homophobic slurs ("That's so gay"). Third, the homophobia of the adults around them frequently limits children's choices: for example, boys are discouraged from wearing fancy dresses or high heels in the dress-up corner because of adults' fears that they will turn out "queer" if they do, or girls are discouraged from high-energy athletics or the carpenter's bench for similar reasons.

Evaluate materials (including books, videos, posters, manipulatives, block play figures), classroom practices, and conversations for these and other homophobic stereotypes:

A. General stereotypes associated with gay men and lesbians:

Gay men:	Lesbians:
passive	short hair
gentle	mannish
neat	gruff
dependent	athletic
limp-wristed	aggressive
overly emotional	tough
overly concerned about fashion and appearance	wear leather
not athletic	ride motorcycles
cross-dressers	walk like men
want to be women	dress like men
pedophiles	want to be men
swishy walk	hate men
promiscuous	tradeswomen
	not feminine: don't wear skirts, lipstick

B. Occupational stereotypes associated with gay men and lesbians:

- Gay men: hairdressers, fashion designers, or interior designers
- Lesbians: tradeswomen, firefighters, police officers, truck drivers, or athletes

C. Stereotypic language and terminology associated with gay men and lesbians:

(Although some of these terms have been reclaimed by gays and lesbians and are being used in positive ways, as a rule, if you are not gay or lesbian, it's better to use the terms *gay, lesbian,* and *sexual orientation.*)

fag	sissy
faggot	butch
queen	dyke
poofter	bulldyke
nellie	lezzie
fairy	homo
queer	homosexual

Use these truths to counteract the stereotypes:

Gay men and lesbians are as diverse as heterosexual men and women. Gay men and lesbians have the same range of sexual activity as heterosexuals. Some have long-term relationships and some do not. Homosexual seduction is far less common than heterosexual seduction. Most gay men, lesbians, and bisexuals, like most heterosexuals, are comfortable with their biological gender.

More than 90 percent of child abuse is committed by heterosexual men who molest young girls. The majority of gay men and lesbians, like the majority of heterosexuals, have no sexual interest in children.

Most lesbians, like most heterosexual women, have male friends, relatives, and colleagues with whom they have relationships varying from amicable to deeply intimate.

People play sports for enjoyment—this is not related to their sexual orientation.

In many cultures two men or two women commonly hug or hold hands with no particular association to homosexuality. Hugging, holding hands, and otherwise being close to someone defines friendship and intimacy, not one's sexuality. Unfortunately, many people limit their expression of affection or their willingness to receive it for fear of being labeled "gay."

Studies show that children raised in gay or lesbian families are no more likely to become gay or lesbian themselves than are children raised in heterosexual families. So even the most visible and constant modeling of homosexuality does not push children into becoming homosexuals themselves.

1. What were the "rules" you had to follow as a child to avoid put-downs (like "fag" or "lezzie") related to homosexuality?

2. List day-to-day ways in which heterosexuality is established as the norm.

3. List daily ways that people around you acknowledge their heterosexuality while people who are gay or lesbian cannot do the same.

4. Discuss the following subjects in relationship to addressing homophobia in the classroom:

   Supporting the self-esteem of children with gay or lesbian parents. As someone who wants the best for each child, how would you support the self-esteem of children who have gay or lesbian parents or family members?

   Finding out what children know about homosexuality and preparing them to respond to bias about gays and lesbians. If you don't have children in your class with gay or lesbian family members and you haven't heard them make comments about sexual orientation, how might you find out what they do know? How might you prepare the children for their inevitable exposure to bias about gays and lesbians?

   Homophobia and friendship. How do you think teasing about being gay affects all friendships for both children and adults? In what other ways does homophobia affect heterosexuals?

   Class meetings. What would a class meeting look like where children and adults discussed homophobic behavior such as the use of the word *gay* as a put-down?

5. Discuss the following scenarios. How do they display bias? How might you respond in the moment? How would you follow up later?

   • Children were gathered around a classroom table involved in an art activity. The conversation led to one child saying, "You can't have two mommies."

   • Two girls were talking and laughing while working closely together. Another child passing by said, "Ooh! They're gay!"

   • Staff are discussing the issue of homosexuality because it has come up in the classroom. Children have been using "gay" as a put-down. In the staff meeting, one of the teachers says, "I have a right to my own beliefs. My religious beliefs say that homosexuality is wrong. Using pictures that include families with gay or lesbian parents goes against those beliefs. I can't read stories with gay or lesbian parents to the children in my classroom."

6. Discuss this statement by Jocelyn Elders, former U.S. surgeon general: "Good parents are good parents, regardless of their sexual orientation. It's clear that the sexual orientation of parents has nothing to do with the sexual orientation or outlook of their children."

7. Do holidays such as Mother's Day, Father's Day, or Valentine's Day perpetuate any stereotypes? For example, consider the stereotype that all women will be or want to be mothers or that all families have a mother and a father. How are children with gay parents affected? How do the holidays promote heterosexism? What goals do you accomplish by the inclusion of Mother's Day and Father's Day in your curriculum? Are there other ways those goals could be accomplished?

8. Discuss the following scenarios. How would you respond? What kind of follow-up would you do?

   • Staff are discussing the issue of family diversity and including stories that have gay and lesbian parents. One of the teachers says, "This isn't an issue for my classroom because none of the children have gay or lesbian parents. I don't feel comfortable bringing in those pictures and stories. And besides, it isn't necessary."

   • A child brings in the story of Snow White and the seven dwarfs and wants you to read it at group story time. Analyze the story using the stereotype lists on sexism and homophobia. Then plan your response to the request to read the book. If you can, use *Walt Disney's Snow White and the Seven Dwarfs* by Rita Balducci (1992) for this exercise.

Sources

Balducci, Rita. 1992. *Walt Disney's Snow White and the seven dwarfs.* Racine, WI: Western.

Clay, James. March 1990. Working with lesbian and gay parents and their children. *Young Children.*

For family and educators of students in grades three through five. A handbook prepared by a committee of students, parents, teachers, and community members representing the diversity of Cambridge, Massachusetts.

Lesbian and Gay Parents Association. 1996. Overcoming homophobia in the elementary classroom: A workshop for educators and administrators, a presenter's guide for use with the video *Both of My Moms' Names Are Judy*. San Francisco: Lesbian and Gay Parents Association.

Thompson, Cooper, and the members of the Campaign to End Homophobia. 1990. A guide to leading introductory workshops on homophobia. Boston.

Chapter 6

Bias Related to Economic Class

Classism is any attitude, action, or institutional practice that subordinates people because of their economic condition. In the United States, dignity and respect are often accorded based on economics. Poor people and members of the working class are not accorded the dignity and respect given to middle-class and wealthy people. In addition, success, status, and "a good life" are defined primarily in terms of material possessions.

One of the great myths of U.S. society has been that we have no class structure, so we don't have a class problem or class conflict. The myth is that anyone who works hard enough can "make it," regardless of one's color or whether one was born rich or poor, or male or female. If some people do possess more than others, they earned it by working hard—or they were lucky. In fact, most people who are born poor, regardless of how hard they work, remain poor. Those who are born rich, regardless of whether or how much they work, remain rich. The single most effective predictor of the socioeconomic class a person ends up in is the socioeconomic class of her parents.

Factory work and other forms of manual labor are generally viewed as inferior to intellectual or professional work, while in reality they are all-important to society. Unless children are taught that all useful work merits respect and a living wage, they will develop into adults who feel they are superior and have a right to look down on others who earn less, or they will become workers who passively accept low status and low pay.

Many books and other media encourage us to wait for luck, magic, or help from some rich or powerful person in order to solve problems.

Fantasy is useful in literature and other media, but not when it encourages escape into the fantastic as a substitute for confronting reality. These messages discourage us from examining problems realistically and acting on them. They make us feel helpless in the face of society's inequities, rather than making us feel we can fight for our beliefs, rights, and a better society for everyone. Conformism implies that the best behavior is "don't rock the boat." Media messages of conformism further discourage us from questioning whether the "usual" way of doing things is best for all people concerned.

Evaluate materials (including books, videos, posters, manipulatives, block play figures), classroom practices, and conversations for these and other class stereotypes:

A. General stereotypes about class:

Rich people:	Poor people:
benevolent	dirty
stingy	lazy
playboy	hardworking
hardworking	honest
pulled themselves up by their bootstraps	incompetent
weak	stupid
clean	foolish, easily misled
healthy	greedy
virtuous	focused on home, family
crooks	sick, unhealthy
smart	vacillating, unfocused
competent	unlucky
good businesspeople	superstitious
indifferent, uncaring	lacking in sense
greedy	tacky or poor taste
focused on status, money, power	generous
determined, iron-willed	irresponsible
lucky	feckless
valuable, important	miserable
sensible	alcoholic
good taste	dysfunctional
ruthless	
happy	

B. Stereotypic story lines associated with economic class:

- A broad range of working people portrayed in positive ways is absent from most children's books, cartoons, and films, as is the world of work in general.

- Workers' feelings about working conditions, the work process, and their relationships to other workers are also absent from most children's stories.

- The portrayal of unemployment and its impact on family life is absent from most children's media.

- Negative value judgments are made or implied about particular kinds of work, especially manual work or the trades.

- The role and importance of common working people in shaping history is absent from most children's media.

- Possession of consumer goods or wealth is the basis for valuing people or valuing oneself.

- Happiness is achieved through the accumulation of possessions.

- Being first or best is worth using any means necessary to get there.

- Messages about sharing and cooperating with others in the community, a positive way of life in many cultures, are often absent.

- Characters are less often valued for their basic qualities (kindness or alertness) and are more often valued for external mannerisms (speech or taste in clothing).

- Royalty or people of the upper classes are most often presented as naturally more desirable, more interesting, or superior to common folk, servants, or working people.

Use these truths to counter the stereotypes:

An institutional system of class privilege in the United States confers opportunity on people unequally according to their class backgrounds. This system is perpetuated by public institutions like schools, banks, courts, and prisons. Although a few people are able to change class, they are the exception rather than the rule, and their stories are often used as a way of justifying or denying the class system (Andrew Carnegie is a classic example)—in other words, if these people can have a rags-to-riches history, then so could anyone who tried hard enough and was smart enough. This is simply not true.

Many rich people don't work at all and remain rich. Many poor people work very hard and remain poor. Many rich people are foolish, superstitious, or incompetent. Many poor people are intelligent, competent, and have good business sense. It is simply not possible to predict a person's intelligence, competence, or common sense based on his or her economic class. Furthermore, what is defined as intelligence, competence, or common sense varies depending on the context.

Material possessions do not guarantee happiness. Similarly, dysfunctional families and addictions such as alcoholism are not related to class. However, poverty creates enormous stresses on individuals and families who do not have access to the basic things they need to survive and thrive: adequate food, clothing, and housing; good education; productive employment and job training; and health care.

The impact of ordinary working people upon history and upon the United States is gigantic and rarely recognized. For one small example, the forty-hour work week and the weekend as we know it today both come from the ceaseless struggle of labor unions in the early part of the twentieth century.

The industrial society depends upon a pool of unemployed workers from which to draw as positions open up and new manufacturing plants are opened.

If we want children to value internal qualities (kindness, generosity, alertness) over external ones (clothes, beauty, material possessions) and to recognize and challenge the injustice in a competitive system that results in inferior services and status for so many, we need to focus less on competition and develop the skills that make possible cooperation based on respect for the experiences, perspectives, and resources we each can contribute.

Discussion Questions and Scenarios

1. Discuss these two statements:

   - "It's not true that whether you start off rich or poor doesn't matter and you can still make it as long as you work hard."

   - "If some people possess more than others, they earned it by working hard."

2. Describe the messages you received as a child about competition. What happened in your daily life that influenced your understanding and experience of competition? What messages do you continue to receive about competition?

3. What are your thoughts on the opposing goals of competition and individual success versus cooperation and group welfare?

4. Discuss this statement: "Rather than valuing individuality—the special qualities of each human being—and making the fulfillment of each person's potential a real possibility, that fulfillment is limited to an elite few." How does it seem true to you? How do you disagree with it? Why?

5. What stereotypical messages did you learn as a child about people who do factory work and other forms of manual labor versus people who do intellectual or professional work? Did anyone or any institution provide an alternative set of messages? How could these messages have been changed?

6. Consider the operation of a major facility or business in your community.

   • Brainstorm a list of all workers responsible for the operation of that institution. Divide the list of workers into two categories labeled "Important" and "Unimportant" as determined by status in our society. List the reasons frequently given for thinking of these workers as unimportant. Are they easily replaced? Do they have limited responsibility? Do their jobs require limited technical ability, limited literacy?

   • What would happen if all of the workers in the "unimportant" list did not come to work for one month?

   • How might the business be restructured if the value in a person's job was not the specific tasks involved, but the recognition of each worker's contribution to the ability of everyone to do his or her job?

7. Discuss this statement: "Many books and other media encourage us to wait for luck, magic, or help from some rich or powerful person in order to solve problems. Fantasy is useful in literature and other media, but not when it encourages escape into the fantastic as a substitute for confronting reality. These messages discourage us from examining problems realistically and then acting on them. They make us feel helpless in the face of society's inequities, rather than making us feel we can fight for our beliefs, rights, and a better society for everyone." What do these ideas have to do with class bias? What do they have to do with anti-bias work with children? Make a list of and talk about books that were read to you as a child or that you now read to children whose solutions to problems rely on luck, magic, or help from a rich or powerful person.

8. Make a list of all the media messages you can think of that encourage conformism. Can you think of any that encourage questioning whether the "usual" way of doing things is best for all people concerned?

9. Discuss your reaction to this statement: "Many of us think that rich people are smarter than poor people rather than perceiving that rich people have simply had more opportunities for education and achievement."

10. Discuss your experiences with class issues related to clothing, either in your own childhood or in your experience as a teacher.

11. What messages do children receive about the importance of newly bought things? Where do these messages come from? How are they conveyed to children?

12. List children's books that counter the consumerism children are routinely exposed to. For example, *The River that Gave Gifts*.

13. Discuss the following scenarios:

   • You're concerned because you and other adults often acknowledge children by remarking on new acquisitions with comments like "I love your new shoes!" Children often say, "See my new dress!" You want to raise this issue and present some suggestions for how to handle material acquisitions differently. How would you present this and what suggestions would you make?

   • You're on a field trip and one of the children sees a homeless man and says, "That man's a bum."

Sources

Bigelow, William, and Norman Diamond. 1988. The power in our hands: A curriculum on the history of work and workers in the United States. New York: Monthly Review Press.

Guidelines for selecting bias-free textbooks and storybooks. 1980. New York: Council on Interracial Books for Children.

Chapter 7

Bias Related to Physical Abilities and Physical Characteristics

Physical Abilities

Ableism is any attitude, action, or institutional practice that subordinates people because of their disability. Ableist institutional practices deny people with disabilities access to mainstream society and keep them socially and economically oppressed. Some of these institutional barriers are physical ones involving the accessibility of public places and worksites; some involve accommodations needed by specific people with disabilities to do specific tasks; and some involve the assumptions of those in power that people with disabilities could not possibly be responsible for running their own lives.

One in every six people in the United States has a physical or developmental disability. For children, the number is one in ten. Most of these children, like most children who do not have disabilities, could grow up to be self-supporting adults—if sufficient funds were used for that purpose, if suitable transportation and access were made available, and if employers were educated to hire people with disabilities. Besides facing these economic oppressions, people with disabilities are stared at, harassed, and insulted.

So many children's "classics" have featured cruel villains who are missing a hand, a leg, or an eye that disability itself has come to connote evil. Many books, films, and cartoons offer "comical" scenes with a Deaf person, a stutterer, or an overweight woman. People with disabilities are often pictured as pathetic, sinister, or interesting primarily because of their disability. Children's books should make young people aware of and concerned about the rights of people with disabilities to work, receive decent pay, have adequate transportation, receive an education, and have a full social life.

Physical Characteristics

Dealing with physical characteristics is sensitive business for young children. Children are often asked to do things like measure themselves or someone else in the class. Children are asked to compare themselves to each other and to a "norm." Children who are particularly tall or particularly short may end up being teased. They are often asked to compare physical skills such as how far they can throw a ball, how far they can jump, or how fast they can run. These comparisons not only create problems for children with diverse physical abilities but also for those who are particularly sensitive about achievement and competition. Therefore, activities that involve measuring, sorting, and comparing, whether for the purpose of discovering similarities and differences or for the purpose of developing math skills, can't be done without a great deal of work on contradicting the stereotypes that judge average-size children as better than larger children, tall as better than short, people without glasses as more attractive than those who have them, or straight hair as better than curly hair.

Sorting by hair texture that places all children of color in the curly hair group—or sorting by eye color that shows all children with blue eyes end up being all white children—serves to emphasize racial differences. Without a corresponding acknowledgment of people's similarities or an active campaign to challenge related bias, the results can easily provide fuel for racist comments.

Evaluate materials (including books, videos, posters, manipulatives, block play figures), classroom practices, and conversations for these and other stereotypes about physical disabilities and physical characteristics:

A. General stereotypes about people with disabilities:

Men with disabilities:	**Women with disabilities:**
evil blind man with unnatural powers	hunchbacked old crone
village idiot	blind witch
evil peg-leg or hook-arm	pitiful blind girl/pitiful little cripple
pitiful paraplegic	sexless sad creature
ugly hunchback	victim of violence
happy moron	

deaf and dumb sad character evil witch with a cane

super cripple/pitiful little cripple self-pitying whiner

childlike dwarf

insane criminal

one-eyed pirate

hard-of-hearing crank

B. Stereotypes related to physical characteristics:

Fat people eat too much.

Thin people eat less than fat people.

Fat people have no self-control.

Thin people are more active than fat people.

It is unhealthy to be fat.

Glasses are unattractive.

Being tall is better than being short.

Boys should be taller than girls.

Straight hair is better than curly hair.

Lighter skin is better than darker skin.

Light (blue, gray, or green) eyes are better than dark eyes.

C. Stereotypic story lines associated with people with physical disabilities:

- People with disabilities are shown as lonesome, unhappy, or in need of help from able-bodied children or adults.

- People with disabilities are often portrayed as beggars, burdens on their families, or unemployed.

- The emphasis is often on what people with disabilities can't do, rather than on the wide range of things they can do.

- People with disabilities are not often characterized as possessing individual and complex personalities, nor as interacting with able-bodied characters based on their individuality, rather than their disability.

- People with disabilities are used for sensationalism to create fear, laughter, pity, or curiosity.

- Story lines often portray people with disabilities in ways that perpetuate misconceptions of what limitations actually exist or do not exist. They promote the idea that people with disabilities are much less capable than they actually are.

- Disabilities are linked to negative personalities, thus perpetuating fear of people who are disabled.

- Special skills or performing superhuman feats allow people with disabilities to be accepted by able-bodied people.

- People with disabilities are presented as happy once they learn to accept their disability and stop pitying themselves. The unhappiness is therefore linked to personal defects rather than to societal barriers to education, transportation, work, and recreation.

- Teasing directed at people who are described as fat often ascribes the problem to an individual's eating habits and the solution as dieting, rather than attempting to expand readers' views on what is normal or attractive.

D. Stereotypic language and terminology associated with people with disabilities and other physical characteristics:

- Negative terms such as *lame, cripple, spastic, retard,* or *idiot* define people based on their disability rather than their full personhood.

- The word *handicap* has been rejected by many disability rights activists because of its historic associations with the "cap-in-hand" begging image.

- There is some criticism of the term *special needs* because it emphasizes a person's neediness.

- Language like "confined to a wheelchair," "suffers from," "afflicted with," and "victim of" reinforces the idea that having a disability is primarily about pain and suffering. It is preferable to use simple factual language like "uses a wheelchair" or "has cerebral palsy."

- Language like "the blind person" defines a person by his or her disability rather than as someone with many interests and abilities who also has a particular disability. It is preferable to put the person first and the disability second: for example, "people with disabilities" or "people who are blind."

- Using words like *brave* or *courageous* implies that one must be a martyr or hero to live with a disability. This reinforces the stereotype of victim. People with disabilities have the full range of attitudes toward life found in able-bodied people.

- The term *person of short stature* is generally preferred to *dwarf*.

- A person is not spastic but has muscles that are spastic.

- The word *seizure* is preferred to *fit*, which has generally derogatory connotations.

- The word *vegetable* should not be used to refer to a person who has lost mental or physical functions.

- *Typical* and *atypical* are preferred to *normal* and *abnormal*. People with disabilities and people with diverse physical characteristics are within the normal range of humanity. They, like everyone else, have things they can do and things they cannot.

- "A person who is unable to speak" or "a person who is non-verbal" is preferred over the word "dumb," which has negative connotations.

- "The blind leading the blind" reinforces an image of people who are blind as helpless or groping and should not be used.

- The phrase *limping along* is often used to describe financial difficulty or to give a negative connotation to moving slowly. This reinforces stereotypes by associating limping with difficulty and not keeping up, as does the use of the word *lame* as pejorative.

- Children who wear glasses are often called "four eyes" and may be harassed by having their glasses grabbed or taken away.

- Fat children are called names like "chubby" and "pig."

- Tall skinny children are called "beanpole."

- Red-haired children are called "carrottop."

- Any other physical characteristic that is turned into a negative nickname is a stereotype.

Use these truths to counteract the stereotypes:

People with disabilities are usually active members of their communities who work, have partners, and raise families. Most people with disabilities lead independent lives. However, physical, economic, and cultural barriers stand in the way of independent living for many people with disabilities who would like to be independent.

Most people with disabilities support themselves and their families. In many cases, people with disabilities who have resorted to begging or who are unemployed would work if not for the bias that denies them relevant work. People with disabilities work at a variety of occupations.

Generally when referring to people with disabilities, show respect by putting the person first and the disability second. For example, use "people with disabilities" not "the handicapped," "man using a wheelchair" not "wheelchair-bound man." Avoid limiting terms such as "confined to a wheelchair." Avoid using "the" in front of an adjective to define a group of people, for example, "the disabled" or "the blind."

While it is commonly implied that people are fat because they eat too much or don't eat the "right" foods, many people who are thin eat just as much and have similar eating habits. It continues to be acceptable in our society to harass and publicly despise fat people. Television shows employ jokes at the expense of fat characters at the average rate of one per show. Fat children often do not receive as much physical contact or affection.

Many studies show that maximum longevity is associated with above-average weight. Obesity is associated with some potentially fatal diseases and also protects against several others. Being too thin is also medically associated with potentially fatal diseases, and also with lowered chances of surviving others.

Discussion Questions and Scenarios

1. Discuss your perspectives on the following terms, including why they might be considered offensive, and develop substitute terms for each:

    Keri is confined to a wheelchair.

    The disabled want their rights.

    Jan suffers from a hearing impairment.

    He is retarded.

    Tyrone is deaf and dumb.

    Shanielle is afflicted with MS.

    You're acting like a retard.

    He's mental.

    That's so lame.

    What a spaz!

    I had a spaz attack.

    Jean Robert had another fit yesterday.

Barbara Ann is a dwarf.

She's a cripple.

Ever since the accident she's been a vegetable.

Reynaldo is spastic.

I work with some children who have disabilities and some who are normal.

Sadie is paralyzed, but she is very courageous.

When Estelle and Simon work together, it's like the blind leading the blind.

Her business is financially limping along right now.

In classrooms for young children, we should include lots of pictures and stories of people who are handicapped.

He's overweight.

2. Discuss the following scenarios. What bias is being expressed? How would you handle it in the moment with the children? What follow-up would you do?

- A group of children were playing with photograph cards. One of the pictures showed a woman in a wheelchair washing a baby in a small tub. The tub was at a height that the woman could easily reach from the wheelchair. When one of the children saw the picture, she said, "People in wheelchairs can't be mommies."

- A child was using a set of people figures that represent all different shapes and sizes. The child looked at one of the figures and said, "Ooh, he's fat! Fat people smell."

Sources

Centers for Independent Living (or "independent living centers"), organizations of and for people with disabilities that provide technical assistance, peer counseling, and advocacy, can often provide information about specific disabilities and about disability rights in general. There is a center in every state.

Everyone Counts. 1985. London, England: Inner London Education Authority Learning Resources Branch.

Education Development Center. Choosing words with dignity. Newton, MA: Education Development Center.

Ernsberger, P., and P. Haskew. Summer 1987. Health implications of obesity: An alternative view. *The Journal of Obesity and Weight Regulation* 6. For more information contact the National

Association to Advance Fat Acceptance, P. O. Box 188620, Sacramento, CA, 95818, or the Full Sun Institute, telephone 503-689-3947.

Whitney, Trisha. May 1995. Respecting body size. *The Web.*

Chapter 8

Bias Related to Race and Ethnicity

Ethnicity, culture, and race are complex and intertwined topics. The words are often used interchangeably, but defining them as separate concepts is essential in understanding racism and bias related to ethnicity and culture.

Ethnicity refers to a person's geographic or national origin, identity, or heritage. Terms such as *African American, European American, Irish American,* and *Mexican American* define ethnicity and refer to a person's ancestral, national, or geographic identity. Ethnicity is inherited.

Culture is defined by the values, traditions, social and political relationships, and worldview shared by a group of people bound together by a combination of commonalities that include one or more of the following: history, geographic location or origin, language, social class, or religion. Culture is learned, not inherited.

Race is a term used to categorize people, usually by skin color and other physical characteristics. The concept of race emerged in the eighteenth century as a justification for colonization and slavery. No biological criteria have ever been established for defining race, yet most people have come to accept the concept of race as if it refers to an objective biological reality. In fact it is a construct designed to separate people from one another and to support the oppression of some people by other people.

Ethnocentrism is the belief that one's own race and ethnic culture are superior to those of others. *Eurocentrism* is the consideration of events and people from the perspective of white people who came to the United States from Europe.

Institutional racism is when the institutional arrangements of a society benefit a particular race at the expense of other races. This can be intentional or unintentional. When one race dominates the major institutions of a society, it has the power to impose its prejudice to the detriment of other races in a way that racial groups without that institutional power cannot do. This is why many people have come to define racism as prejudice plus power. Anyone can be prejudiced, but not everyone who is prejudiced has institutional advantage—the power to subordinate people based on race.

For example, white people who immigrated to the United States had a big advantage when it came to making and saving money, compared to African American people and other people of color. African Americans were not able to begin accumulating money in this society until slavery was abolished, and other people of color faced similar restrictions. Today we see this reflected in many institutions, such as in higher education. The ability to work and earn money allowed white people to send their children to college. That education led to better jobs, which led to more money being passed down and allowing the next generation of children and grandchildren to attend college as well. The result is institutional racism: White people dominate in higher education institutions—both as students and as those able to obtain professional jobs within the institutions. That dominance led to defining what would be taught, how success would be measured, and who else could get in.

Racism and ethnocentrism present special difficulties, particularly for those of us who are white, in recognizing and understanding their manifestations and complexities. Most of us who are white think of ourselves as nonracist—and many of us want to be anti-racist. The notion that we may unintentionally be perpetuating racism is often extremely difficult to accept. It feels like an attack on our self-image as good people.

It is therefore often a lot easier to let down some of the defenses and begin to examine how racism works if we repeatedly remind ourselves that, for most of us, racism is not about being a bad person. It's about absorbing, without knowing it, a tremendous body of misinformation, attitudes, values, and behaviors from the environment, which takes intentional work to understand and change.

Evaluate materials (including books, videos, posters, manipulatives, block play figures), classroom practices, and conversations for these and other racist and ethnocentric stereotypes:

A. General stereotypes associated with people of color:

African Americans

Men:

shuffling, eye-rolling, fearful, superstitious comic

gentle, self-sacrificing older man

athletic superjock

smooth-talking con man

superstud

stupid, but comical, little boy

rough, dangerous criminal

loudly dressed, happy-go-lucky buffoon

exotic primitive

Women:

big-bosomed mammy, loyal to whites

big, bossy mother or maid, commander of the household

sexy temptress

stupid, but sweet, little girl

Latinos/Latinas

Men:

wearing sombreros

serape-clad

wearing sandals

taking siesta near cactus, under a tree, or near an overburdened burro

ignorant, cheerful, lazy peon

sneaky, knife-wielding, mustached bandit

humble, big-eyed, poor-but-honest boy

teenage gang member

Women:

hard-working, poor, submissive, self-sacrificing religious mother of many

sweet, small, shy, gentle girl

sexy, loud, fiery, young woman

undereducated, submissive, nice girl

Asian Americans

Men:	**Women:**
smiling, polite, small, servile, bowing	sweet, well-behaved girl
bucktoothed and squinty-eyed	shy
mystical, inscrutable, and wise	smiling
expert in martial arts	dainty
cruel, sneaky, sinister, sly, evil	sexy, sweet ("China Doll")
superstudent	sexy, evil ("Dragon Lady")
places no value on human life	overbearing, old-fashioned grandmother
model minority who worked hard and made it	

Native Americans

Men:	**Women:**
bloodthirsty, stoic, loyal follower	heavyset, workhorse
drunken, mean thief	"Indian princess" depicted with European features, often in love with a white man for whom she is willing to sacrifice her life
drunken comic	
stealthy hunter-tracker	
noble child of nature	obedient, submissive "squaw"
wise old chief	
evil medicine man	
brave boy, endowed by nature with special "Indian" qualities	

B. Occupational stereotypes associated with people of color:

African Americans:

chauffeur

cook

maid

laundry worker

elevator operator

waiter

unemployed ghetto-dweller

preacher

undertaker

athlete

entertainer

Latinos/Latinas:

campesino (rural farm worker)

migrant farm worker

unemployed barrio dweller

Asian Americans:

Chinese American men:

laundry worker

restaurant worker

curio shop owner

railroad worker

Japanese American men:

gardener

florist

Filipino American men:

houseboy

Native Americans:

hunter

cattle thief

warrior

unemployed loafer

craftsperson

shaman

Notes about stereotyping of people of color: Many of these stereo-types are based on historical and current racism, which relegate people of color to particular occupations and continue to keep them in the same low-paying or otherwise restricted occupations. It is vital that children be given the information that occupations are not linked to race or ethnicity, but are often affected by bias. For example, slavery restricted African Americans to menial positions, and current racism continues to keep a disproportionate number of African Americans in the same low-paying jobs. In the past, racism allowed Asian Americans to work only in a limited number of occupations, such as cooking or laundry work, which most white male workers spurned as being "unmanly." Even today, many Chinese Americans can find work only in the kitchens of Chinese restaurants or in garment sweatshops. In addition, watch out for the portrayal of the Asian American experience as a "success" story. This gives the false impression that Asian Americans have overcome the oppression against them by hard work and passively turning the other cheek. Asian Americans are often presented as a model for other groups to emulate. This creates tension among groups as well as extreme pressure on Asian Americans to live up to the expectations of the stereotype.

C. Stereotypical story lines related to race and ethnicity:

- There is an underrepresentation of both males and females of color portrayed as positive role models. The people of color who are highlighted are often those who show preferences for white culture and white characters.

- During interplay between white characters and people of color, the viewpoints of the people of color are often not as clear as are viewpoints and values of white characters.

- People of color are likely to be the disposable characters in a majority of movies and cartoons, giving the impression that people of color are less important. A character of color is often sacrificed to save a white person.

- A person from the nondominant culture must give up some aspect of her root culture in order to achieve happiness or success.

- A character of color is often portrayed as more concerned about a white character than about other characters.

- A person of color is often portrayed as seeking to be accepted by whites. Characters often have to show extraordinary attributes or perform extraordinary feats in order to win acceptance by whites, rather than being respected on their own terms.

- A benevolent white person solves a problem for a person of color, implying that people of color are less capable than whites.

- The color white is overwhelmingly used in a positive context, while black is overwhelmingly used in a negative context.

- Standard English is portrayed as inherently better than other forms of English or than other languages.

- "Broken English," stilted speech, or parodies of speech patterns are used in a demeaning way to portray a person whose first language is not English. For example, Native Americans are often portrayed as grunting or saying "How" or "Many moons ago, me come."

- All members of a group are portrayed as living in set places, working in like occupations, or having similar socioeconomic status. For example, Mexican Americans are portrayed as farm workers. While many Mexican Americans are farm workers, many more live and work in urban environments.

- The viewpoint is often that of a white person looking at the culture of a person of color, rather than the viewpoint of someone from within the culture. The viewpoint of a person of color looking at the behavior of white characters is rarely included. Few stories depict the realistic experiences and feelings of children and adults of color that come from living in a racist society.

- The oppression faced by many racial and ethnic groups is often omitted. For example, the internment of Japanese Americans in concentration camps during World War II is rarely mentioned. Such current problems as unemployment, violations of Native fishing rights, and police brutality in communities of color are rarely reflected in stories or other information for children. Incidents of racial prejudice are often presented as isolated acts, rather than as typical of what constantly occurs in the lives of people of color in U.S. society.

- People of color are shown accepting their inferior status, often by eliminating the perspective of the people fighting the oppression. Even when the oppression itself is described, the struggle against it is left out of the story.

- People of color are often blamed for their own difficulties, rather than societal causes such as the racism of the dominant white society. The strengths and supportive characteristics of families of color are often not shown. Rather, there is an emphasis on their problems, which are often blamed on the family itself rather than on societal issues such as racism and discrimination.

- Learning "good" English is presented as the solution to social problems such as poverty and inferior education.

- History is often portrayed from the viewpoint of what was advantageous to whites or how events appeared to whites. For example, Native American victories are most often described as *massacres,* while the indiscriminate killing, extermination, and plunder of Native American nations by European Americans is described as *victory.*

- People of color are often portrayed for what they have done for whites, rather than for what they have done for their own people. For example, Native Americans are congratulated for giving the settlers help in surviving the early winters by teaching them how to grow corn. But how did the domestication of corn help Native American societies?

- Heroes from nondominant ethnic communities are most often highlighted as such because they supported U.S. interests rather than because they are considered to be heroes by their own people. In most cases, the contributions to society of nondominant racial and ethnic groups receive little or no credit.

- Viewpoints and events critical of U.S. policies or actions are often omitted when they might logically be included.

- Groups are often presented in simplistic, and therefore inaccurate, ways by relying on material objects associated with them, such as pottery, homes, and jewelry. A few customs are used to represent a group, thus trivializing what is a complex system of values and beliefs. For example, sand paintings, a sacred ritual, may be presented as an interesting art project. In addition, totally different ethnic groups, lifestyles, clothing, and homes are jumbled together in one African, Latino, Native, or Asian stereotype, rather than depicting the enormous diversity of cultures.

- Folktales from the nondominant culture are often distorted when white writers apply them to European American concepts, thereby losing or changing the original meaning.

- Settings, behavior, speech, and clothing are not depicted accurately for the historical period or cultural context. For example, traditional Chinese and Japanese garments, rarely worn by contemporary Asian Americans, are nonetheless associated with them; many of the Brer Rabbit stories were about slaves tricking their masters, not just cute animal stories.

- The culture and values of some ethnic groups are portrayed as unsuited to modern, technological society, rather than suggesting that dominant U.S. culture might learn from the values and belief systems of others.

- Full reasons for immigration to the United States are rarely presented. Excluding information about harsh conditions in immigrants' countries of origin (often exacerbated by U.S. foreign policy) or active recruitment by U.S. business interests leads children and adults to believe that people from ethnic groups in other countries have come to the United States simply to "get rich quick."

- People of color from various parts of the world are depicted as placing much less value on human life than the dominant culture in the United States does. This is seen as ironic by many people of color given the genocide of Native Americans in this country, the dropping of the atomic bomb on Hiroshima and Nagasaki, and the 200,000 people who were killed by U.S. forces during the first Gulf War and the hundreds of thousands who continue to die from its aftereffects.

D. Stereotypical language and terminology related to race and ethnicity:

Native Americans:
buck

squaw

papoose

heathen

primitive

wild

furtive

savage

stealthy

skulking

comparison to animals: eyes like a fox, untamed as a wolf

Asian Americans:
inscrutable

Other loaded terms:

- *discover:* This word is frequently used to describe European voyages to places they had not previously been, as in the phrase, "Columbus discovered America." Discover is defined as "to gain sight or knowledge of something previously unseen or unknown." The use of this word to describe white encounters with people of color on their land is thus ethnocentric, since it shows the situation from only the European point of view. Imagine travelers who had not previously visited the United States stepping off a plane and saying they had "discovered" America—a continent inhabited by millions of human beings cannot be discovered.

- *minority:* This has the connotation of "less than." It is also inaccurate, since in the world as a whole people of color vastly outnumber white people.

- *uncivilized:* This term is so relative as to be completely unclear. Who determines what *civilization* is? Is civilization equated with technology? When the term is repeatedly applied to poorer nations with mostly people of color by nations whose dominant groups are white, the term takes on racist connotations.

- *underdeveloped:* The use of this term implies that there is an ideal stage of development that a group, culture, or nation has not yet reached, and it ignores the fact that the level of development of the United States is not sustainable for the world as a whole, since it depends on the United States consuming the resources of other poorer countries. It also suggests that the nation being described (generally a nation of people of color) is in poor circumstances because of its own lack of development rather than because it's a victim of exploitation by the primarily white-controlled governments, financial institutions, and corporations of Europe and the United States.

- *nonwhite:* This defines people in terms of whiteness. White remains the norm against which to measure others.

- racial epithets such as *Jap, gook, chink,* and *nigger:* Like the use of the terms *boy* and *girl* to describe adult males and females of color, particularly African Americans, these are not common in new materials but still appear in old books in libraries and old films shown repeatedly on television. In these contexts, they are often used without the clarification that they are offensive.

- qualifiers such as *intelligent, articulate,* and *qualified:* Words that would normally have positive connotations can have negative connotations when used in a racial context. For example, "In Atlanta, the president met with a group of articulate African American leaders." It is unlikely that the word "articulate" would be used to describe a group of white leaders—their competence would be assumed.

- *names:* These can be inaccurate and misleading in many ways. For example, multicultural "quotas" are often filled by giving characters ethnically diverse names while in other ways the character seems to be a member of the dominant culture. Sometimes characters of color aren't given names at all or are referred to by first name only. Furthermore, names of characters from nondominant races and cultures are often inauthentic and demeaning parodies of real names: the Lone Ranger called his Native American companion Tonto, which in Spanish, commonly spoken in areas where the episodes of the story take place, means "fool." Finally, names often reflect those given by the dominant culture and not the correct names of people in their own cultures and families. For example, Sitting Bull is Totanka Iotanka; Crazy Horse is Tashunka Witko.

- *we, us,* and *people:* These terms are often used to refer solely to whites. For example, "The people watched the slaves work" implies slaves are not people.

- *native:* This word develops racist connotations when repeatedly applied to people of color. White people are native to Europe, but rarely are referred to as *natives.*

- *tribe:* This term is often used exclusively in relation to Africa or Africans and never applied to Europeans. Conflicts among diverse peoples within African nations are often referred to as "tribal warfare," while conflicts among the diverse peoples of European countries, like those between the Serbs and Slavs in Yugoslavia, are not.

- *jungle, hut:* Words such as *jungle* or *hut* acquire racist connotations when they are constantly associated with people of color and terms like *uncivilized* and *primitive.* Many people are replacing *jungle* with *wooded savanna. Hut* is best replaced by terms like *home* or *dwelling,* preceded by *temporary.*

E. Stereotypes in illustrations that relate to race and ethnicity:

- People of color are often underrepresented relative to their percentage of the population. In addition, they often appear as tokens—just one or two. Often, they are not illustrated as prominently as whites, but are placed in the background or at the edges of the picture. They are infrequently shown in leadership positions, particularly those that include directing or leading white people.

- Facial characteristics and hairstyles often reflect white faces and styles simply changed in color. Or characteristics and hairstyles are exaggerated and stereotypic. For example, Asians are portrayed with slits and slants instead of eyes.

- Racial or ethnic diversity within a group is often not depicted. All people from the diverse Asian or Latin American countries do not look alike.

- Socioeconomic status and lifestyles are not illustrated in as varied ways as they are for whites.

- Stereotypic props are used to establish ethnic identity. For example, feathers, tepees, braids, and beads are often used to signal to the reader that a character is Native American, whether or not these are appropriate to the story, the tribe, the time period, or the individual character. Similarly, kimonos, dragons, kites, and paper lanterns are used to signal that a character is Asian or Asian American, whether or not these items are culturally relevant or relevant to the individual or to the story.

- Clothing is often unsuitable for the occasion and is also often used as a prop to establish ethnic identity. For example, sombreros are used to connote Mexicans or Mexican Americans and kimonos are used to depict Japanese or Japanese Americans, even though these items are rarely used by contemporary Mexican Americans and Japanese Americans.

- Peoples' lives are often depicted in the past rather than the present. This is one reason why many young children think that Native Americans, in particular, no longer exist.

- Illustrations often rely on special holiday celebrations rather than on daily life.

- Poor ethnic neighborhoods are often portrayed as stereotypically charming, gay, and colorful postcardlike places.

- Native Americans are the only human beings used in the same ways as animals or objects, particularly in alphabet and counting books. Many of these contain such constructions as "Nine foolish hens, Ten red Indians" and "I is for ice cream, ink, and Indian."

Discussion Questions and Scenarios

1. What are some of your earliest memories of learning about skin color?

2. When did you first recognize yourself to be a member of a racial group? Describe what led up to that. How did you feel and what did you think about that identification?

3. Many adults think that young children don't notice skin color. What do you think about this?

4. What's the problem with repeated story lines in which a person of color seeks to be accepted by whites? What's the problem with repeated story lines in which whites accept a person of color after she or he performs extraordinary feats?

5. Why are there objections to repeated story lines in which a white person solves problems faced by people of color? Isn't it a good thing to help other people?

6. What's the problem with repeated story lines in which people of color are portrayed for what they have done for whites rather than for what they have done for their own people?

7. What do you think about objections to illustrations and dramas in which children play "Indian"?

8. Talk about the difficulties with the following terms. Can you think of substitute terms?

    nonwhite

    minority

    underdeveloped

    uncivilized

9. Replace the following words and phrases used in relation to Native Americans with nonderogatory ones:

    buck

    squaw

    papoose

10. What's the problem in these sentences? Can you rewrite them?

    • "In Atlanta, the president met with a group of articulate African American leaders."

    • "The southern students did not want to be called 'rednecks.'"

    • "Work at a local shoe factory that used to be done by Chinese immigrants is now done by Bostonians."

11. The word *tribe* is often used to describe people in Africa, and *tribal warfare* to describe their battles. What's the problem and how could you change it?

12. Many adults say that they are color-blind—that they don't notice race—and they treat everyone as human beings. What are your thoughts on the concept of being "color-blind?"

13. Consider the following statement:

In choosing books and photographs, we make choices about what diversity to include in our classrooms. We begin by reflecting children in the class. We expand to include people whom the children are likely to come into direct contact with as they get older. We expand to include people whom the children will develop ideas and attitudes about even though they may never actually meet.

How is this statement reflected/not reflected in your current collection of books and poster displays?

14. Racial issues don't affect all children in the same way, but they do affect all children, regardless of racial background or the racial composition of one's classroom, school, or community. In what ways are the children in your program affected by racial issues?

15. How might you think about addressing bias about race or ethnicity even before it comes up in the classroom?

16. Can you think of mistakes you've made when attempting to include materials reflecting racial diversity in your classroom?

17. Discuss the following scenarios. How might you handle them in the moment? What would you do to follow up later? Role-play the scenarios.

- A child is playing with a big puzzle on the rug. Another child decides she wants to play too. The first child, who wants to play alone, says, "No, you can't play cuz your skin is brown." The injured child comes to you and says, "She won't let me play with her cuz I'm brown." How would you respond?

- A teacher is sitting with some children who are painting at a table. You overhear the teacher say, "Don't mix all those beautiful colors together. It will come out all brown."

- A child is looking at several pictures that the teacher said are Native people or Indians. She picks up one of them and says, "They're not real Indians. Real Indians wear feathers."

- Children have seen repeated newscasts on television about starvation in Africa. They don't really know where Africa is, just that it's a place and the people who live there or go there are in danger of dying from not having enough food. Children are talking about Africa while drawing pictures at the art table. You hear a child say, "People in Africa don't have enough food so they die." You know that there is famine in some parts of Africa. But Africa is a huge place of more than fifty countries with many prosperous rural areas and big modern cities. You know that cartoons and movies provide children with a lot of stereotypes about Africa. And you know that many African Americans want their children to feel pride in their African heritage.

- A child sees a picture of a baby being carried in a basket and says, "Babies don't go in baskets."

Source

Guidelines for selecting bias-free textbooks and storybooks. 1980. New York: Council on Interracial Books for Children.

Chapter 9

Classroom Strategies for an Anti-Bias Approach

Each of the strategies listed below can be used to respond to all or many of the issues of bias covered by the chapters in this book. Use this list to help answer the question, "What strategies could I use or adapt to deal with the biases raised in each chapter?"

1. Books and commercially available materials.

Identify books or commercially available materials, such as puzzles, puppets, music, or games, that are relevant to the issues in a given chapter. Choose one or more of these materials for each of the following categories:

- Unbiased or anti-biased messages and information through illustrations, story lines, and role models.

- Opportunities to discuss fairness and models for challenging unfairness

- Opportunities to critique bias.

- Opportunities to adapt or change stories to reflect more diverse or complex perspectives or to model responding to bias. For example, in *The Three Little Pigs,* by changing the wolf to an elephant who floods the brick house with water you could change the messages that hard work is the reason for success and laziness is the reason for failure, and that homes of brick are the best. Or you could create a dialogue in *Angel Child, Dragon Child* that models challenging bias about language.

2. Photographs.

Think of particular photographs you could use related to each chapter. List specific sources of photographs you know of.

- How can you use photographs in ways that would elicit children's ideas about a specific type of bias? challenge related bias? provide new information?

- Think of ways you might adapt math, language, and other developmental activities for use with photographs (for example, counting, comparing, and adding the number of people in diverse families).

3. Curriculum themes and learning experiences designed to counter bias.

Think of ways to integrate issues related to bias into relevant curriculum themes:

- A theme on the languages we speak or the way we communicate could include sign language and Braille.

- Bath time for dolls can be used to show that color doesn't wash off.

4. Change character names in stories.

Think of stories that show males or females in nontraditional roles. Use gender-neutral names for the characters (Chris, Pat, Alex), and read the stories without showing the pictures. Then invite children to draw or describe the characters. Ask questions to elicit their thoughts, and discuss why they thought the characters were male or female.

Adapting this strategy, think of stories you could read or create with characters who do not fit stereotypes. Invite children to draw or describe the characters. Ask questions to elicit their impressions, discuss why they think certain characters might be young/old, male/female, able-bodied/physically challenged, wealthy or middle-class/working-class or poor, white/person of color, or of a particular ethnic background.

5. Complicate simplistic thinking.

Help children move beyond the rigidity of seeing things as purely good or evil based on certain visible characteristics, such as skin color, height, or weight. Use questions to help children expand their thinking. For example, think of opportunities for the following scenarios:

- What open-ended questions could you ask to find out children's current information and ideas about the issues raised in this chapter?

- Can you think of a particular situation in which you used or could have used open-ended questions to encourage critical thinking about bias related to this chapter? Give details.

- Assist children to see the ways people in any group can be simultaneously similar and different. For example, talk about ways families are similar and different.

- Assist children to see ways they are similar to people who have notable differences from them.

6. Class meetings.

Have you ever tried a class meeting? Are there current issues related to a given chapter that you might like to talk about in a class meeting? How might the issue be introduced? What concerns do you have about bringing it up?

7. Family or community stories.

Are there family or community stories that you could collect related to an area of bias?

8. Problem-solving stories using role-playing, puppets, persona dolls, or drawings.

Create a persona doll or puppet story that reflects a situation relevant to an area of bias and illustrates a problem that children could talk about and develop possible solutions for. The story could be based on a real issue you are currently facing in your classroom relevant to the area of bias. A good reference for using persona dolls to explore issues around bias is *Kids Like Us* by Trisha Whitney (Redleaf Press, 1999).

- Think of specific displays, games, play figures, or other materials you might create that reflect how children would respond in a situation involving bias.

- Ask children to make drawings that illustrate a problem related to bias.

9. Field trips.

Think of field trips that would provide exposure to anti-bias information related to a given chapter. For example, trips into diverse neighborhoods where children would hear unfamiliar languages and see unfamiliar people.

10. Guests.

What relevant guests, community workers, or family members could you invite to your classroom?

11. Stereotype or fact.

Prepare a series of statements related to a topic from one of the chapters. Ask children to decide whether the statement is stereotype or fact. For example, "Boys can run faster than girls. Stereotype or fact?"

12. Word of the week.

Choose a word or phrase each week related to one of the chapters. Think of ways to use the word or phrase in daily activities.

13. Bias in popular media; comparing stereotypes to reality.

Think of specific forms of media that young children are exposed to that perpetuate the bias raised in a specific chapter. What strategies might you use in the classroom to respond?

Help children make comparisons between reality and stereotypical images from various forms of media. For example, compare a drawing of a Native American wearing feathers and sitting cross-legged in front of a tepee to pictures of Native people engaged in a wide variety of present-day activities.

14. Activism.

Make a list of and follow up on specific opportunities to act against unfairness in response to current classroom or community issues relevant to the lives of children in your program.

15. What additional strategies have you tried or can you think of?

Appendices

A. Guidelines for Facilitators

B. Checklist for Creating and Assessing Anti-Bias Environments

C. Ten Quick Ways to Analyze Children's Books for Sexism and Racism

D. Photograph Games for an Anti-Bias Approach

E. Guidelines for Challenging Racism and Other Forms of Oppression

F. Practice Responding to Bias

G. Resources for an Anti-Bias Approach

Appendix A

Guidelines for Facilitators

This appendix is intended to assist facilitators in leading group discussions involving the *Start Seeing Diversity* book and/or video. If you are able to show the *Start Seeing Diversity* video to the group, we encourage you to show it multiple times for greatest effectiveness. Otherwise, the guidelines below will help facilitators lead discussions of the book and its application to their classrooms.

Using the Video

We recommend that facilitators using the *Start Seeing Diversity* video show a section of the video at a time, with discussion following. It is also helpful to give participants the opportunity to see the entire video more than once. While it is possible to view the video in one sitting, it is our experience that a single viewing does not allow viewers to benefit from all that it contains. Even the advisory committee of experienced teachers, trainers, and administrators, which met month after month to view and discuss the video, found new insights with each viewing. It was certainly my own experience, in reading *Anti-Bias Curriculum: Tools for Empowering Young Children,* that I simply needed to set aside whole pieces I was not yet ready to integrate into my thinking or practice. With each subsequent review of the book or portions of it, I was repeatedly surprised by the treasure I found that I had earlier been unable to appreciate. People have expressed similar experiences with the *Start Seeing Diversity* video.

In fact, there is a potential danger in using the video in a single showing—the possibility that viewers will fall prey to the "been there, done that" syndrome. Unfortunately, it is often difficult to know how much we don't know as we enter new areas of knowledge and practice. Culturally relevant anti-bias work is a process—a long-term course of growing awareness and deeper complexity of understanding—not a one-shot "I got it" kind of thing. Based on our own process of discovery, we strongly recommend that viewing the video not be limited to a one-time session. We suggest viewing it as a whole, and then reviewing it section by section, with ample time after each viewing for discussion and experimentation. The facilitator's guidelines that follow include some strategies and tools for that method.

We suggest beginning with the introduction, since it lays the foundation for the rest of the video with the four anti-bias goals and the eight assumptions that underlie our work at Washington-Beech. However, the sections on specific areas of bias may be viewed in any order, depending on what is most relevant to your group or program at the time.

Group Discussion Formats

Each chapter of this book addressing a particular bias corresponds to a section of the *Start Seeing Diversity* video and provides a series of suggested questions, exercises, and helpful readings. Depending on your circumstances, you may choose to vary the format of the discussion. If you have a relatively large group, you may want to stay together in one group for some exercises and at other times choose a format that provides more opportunities for each person to participate. Here are some examples of formats that have worked well for us:

- Discussions can take place in small groups of two, three, four, or five people.

- You may want to begin in pairs and then have each pair join with another pair for the next question.

- You can have people keep the same partners for the whole session, or trade partners every question, or something in between. It's generally best to change partners at least once, to provide a variety of interactions.

- You may have small groups bring back particularly important points or difficult issues to the larger group. You might have each group write major ideas on easel paper and post them for others to look at.

- You might want to try using concentric circles. Form two circles with the same number of people in each, one inside the other. Have the people in the inner circle face out and the people in the outer circle face in. Each person from the outside circle should be paired with a person on the inside. Participants can discuss the first question in these pairs. Then have the inner circle rotate to the left or right so new pairs are formed. After each question one of the circles rotates again, giving participants the opportunity to talk with a variety of people.

- Offer groups the option to present their responses in the form of role-playing. In discussions there is sometimes a tendency to talk about the incident but not get to specific responses. Role-playing helps to focus on practicing specific responses. Role-playing is also helpful in working through the scenarios that are included in each chapter's discussion questions. Some people are very resistant to role-playing. You can handle this resistance by making role-playing optional. Then ask those who are reluctant or unwilling to join in to help in ways other than taking on a specific role.

- It is also possible to set the scenarios in a fish bowl. A group seated in the middle acts out the scenario. This can be repeated several times with observers allowed to step in during the action and replace one of the participants. This approach can quickly provide a variety of responses, which can then be discussed by the whole group.

These are only a few suggestions for varying the format in ways that will appeal to different styles within your group. You probably have your own ideas for successful strategies.

Keeping a Log

We recommend that during the sessions the facilitator keep an ongoing log of comments and events that are relevant to anti-bias work or to the *Start Seeing Diversity* book and/or video. These may include scenarios from classrooms, interactions between staff, interactions with parents and other family members, or things you notice in the world beyond your programs. They may include raising questions about, or taking notice of, bias in various forms of media, such as television programming and commercials, movies, plays, music, or books, as well as interactions you're involved in or see in the course of each day. Adding these observations to the scenarios provided in the book and/or the video will enhance the relevance of the process for everyone involved. Facilitators may keep a log themselves or ask participants to do so, or both.

Strategies for Using the Scenarios

"Responding to Incidents Involving Bias" and "Guidelines for Challenging Racism and Other Forms of Oppression," both found in the following appendices, will assist participants in thinking through all the elements of each scenario and in constructing possible responses.

In discussing each of the scenarios, use the following questions:

1. What happened? Describe your reaction and those of others.

2. Why did it happen? If you didn't react, why not?

3. What was the impact of what happened?

4. What was done/could be done to change what happened? What could have been done differently? In analyzing this question consider the following:

- What does the response accomplish?

- Is there a conflict between your own beliefs and those of other adults or families of children involved? How was that conflict resolved? Is the response respectful of the different beliefs involved?

- Did the questions model investigation rather than interrogation that embarrassed or shamed? Did the questions encourage critical thinking and reflection on new and old information?

- Did the group

  —address relevant developmental issues?

  —affirm the feelings and identity of each person?

  —provide necessary new information?

  —build on an understanding of "fairness"?

  —build on relevant models for activism?

  —empower the victim?

  —address issues other than bias?

Leading Difficult Discussions

It's important to remember that for many people the discussion, book, and video will be providing new information. Some may feel a resistance to information that shakes their view of the world around them. They may raise contradictory experiences to refute the existence or the broad impact of oppression and discrimination. There may be turbulent disagreement.

In addition, we know that discussions about topics such as race, gender, class, sexual orientation, ethnicity, and other identities that are the target of bias can be difficult. They can bring up strong feelings and opinions. They can bring out the unintentional expression of bias that may offend other participants or result in feedback that creates defensiveness or hurt feelings.

When this happens, it's crucial that you don't let a stereotype or comment containing bias stand. Either facilitate discussion so the group can respond, or explain what is biased. A big part of the work in the anti-bias approach is examining our own misconceptions. Everyone needs outside help to do that sometimes. In addition, bias and stereotypes hurt people. If the stereotype or the expression of bias goes unchallenged, it jeopardizes the quality of the session for anyone in the group who was the subject of the bias, and for anyone who fears that his or her group may become the subject of stereotypes and other forms of bias.

It may be helpful to remind participants that while stereotypes have a basis in reality, they distort reality as well, because they attribute characteristics to a group of people that might define some individuals some of the time but do not apply to all or even most people in that group. So the fact that something is a stereotype doesn't mean that it is never true of an individual, only that it is unfairly applied to a whole group.

We also suggest you avoid exercises that ask participants simply to list biases or stereotypes without also explicitly characterizing these statements as untrue or truth-distorted.

It's helpful to think about potential tough spots as a group before actually getting into the discussions. Below is an initial list of tough spots and hints for navigating difficult discussions. It has proven helpful to review and talk about this list before beginning discussion.

Some Helpful Tips for Difficult Discussions

Each of us is from many cultures. We each have an ethnic culture; others resulting from racial, class, and gender distinctions; and still others based on sexual orientation, age, religious affiliation, or physical ability. There are many similarities and differences across these cultures, and many difficult issues of bias, advantage, and inequity inevitably come up in our interactions with others in ways that we are unaware of. In tackling some of these issues it can be helpful to acknowledge some common "tough spots." Awareness of them can make negotiating some of the tensions a little easier.

Discussion Guidelines

Discuss the guidelines below. Which ones do you find helpful? Which do you have questions about? Do some of them need to be adapted or changed to be culturally relevant or otherwise meet the needs of the group? Are there things you would add?

1. Accept that what's "in your face" obvious to some may be utterly invisible to others.

Those of us who don't see an offense are not stupid or mean. Most of us are simply unequipped to do so. We have been bombarded by misinformation. Most of us are products of an educational system and life experience dominated by singular perspectives that have not prepared us to be open to or even aware of diverse perspectives or to be critical observers and thinkers.

2. Use a word like "ouch" or "time-out" or some other mechanism to stop the action.

Many difficult issues of bias, advantage, and inequity inevitably come up in our interactions with others. It is helpful for the group to agree upon a mechanism that group members can use to signal when one of these issues has surfaced, so the issue can get some attention. Some groups use a word like *ouch* to stop the action.

3. Recognize that bias is not our fault.

Having bias pointed out is no reflection on whether someone is a good person. It's about being responsive to the feedback—really listening—and reevaluating our own thoughts and behaviors.

4. Understand that bias is not about intent— it's about impact.

We usually don't mean to offend or hurt another person, so often our response is to keep on insisting, "But I didn't mean it to be offensive. . . ." If something reflects bias, whether we mean it to or not, it does hurt, and it is not okay. Our defensiveness often makes things worse. Not only have we offended someone, but then we argue with them about whether the offense is real or not, since we didn't mean it that way!

5. Listen actively to one another.

Listening means turning off the doubting and defending mechanisms long enough to really understand (and that can take a while!). It can mean rephrasing to see if we understood, or asking clarifying questions. Those of us who don't see the bias that another person is experiencing can listen and take advantage of the precious opportunity when someone is willing and able to share his or her experience with us. Begin with the assumption that alternative thoughts, ideas, opinions, and behaviors have something to offer and are therefore worth giving serious consideration.

Where there appears to be disagreement, it is often helpful to ask sincere questions to better understand the perspectives of others. Questions do not reflect stupidity. They are an important way to get new information.

6. Allow for diverse conversational styles.

Diverse conversational styles may require some thoughtful negotiation. Some people feel that a dynamic discussion means participants interrupt each other, more than one person talks at once, and it's okay to use a loud voice. Others feel the exact opposite and expect one person to speak at a time, each speaker to wait until the other has finished, the facilitator to call on people who raise their hands, and people's voices to remain low and steady.

People whose style it is to wait until another speaker finishes often have difficulty finding the appropriate moment to speak in a group where others are comfortable interrupting or talking simultaneously. They may view such a dynamic style of discussion as argumentative—raising the fear of hurt feelings or of decisions being made in the heat of emotion.

On the other hand, responses that seek to limit expressiveness or argument can be viewed as inhibiting, even disrespectful. People can feel stifled by waiting until each speaker is finished, hand-raising, and modulating tone and volume.

A person whose style is direct may get impatient with someone whose style is indirect. A person whose style is indirect may be offended by someone whose style is direct.

It is important not to dismiss these and other differences as simply differences in style. We need to become more aware of our own styles and preferences, and of how these influence our interactions and our perceptions of the discussions we are in.

7. Expect disagreement and practice conflict management.

Some people are relatively comfortable with disagreement and argument, while others are not. Disagreement in some form is inevitable where there are diverse views and experiences—but disagreement doesn't mean disrespect. Conflicts may be unsettling to some group members, but often it is more important to acknowledge the conflict that exists and explore the differing perspectives than it is to try to resolve the conflict.

8. Acknowledge that the feelings, opinions, and ideas of others may be painful.

Dealing with issues related to racism, sexism, or classism may lead to the expression of feelings, opinions, and ideas that can be painful to hear. Hearing a bias expressed about one's own group or being told that one has just unintentionally expressed a bias about someone else's group can be painful.

We can manage the normal tension in these situations more easily if we do our best to avoid expressing concerns in ways that attack or blame. Asking questions that help someone reconsider his or her ideas can often be helpful. Beginning statements with "I feel/think" rather than starting sentences with "you" can also help by sounding less blaming and judgmental. This means simultaneously taking the risk to say difficult things to each other and being as thoughtful as possible in how we say those things. This difficult balance does not necessarily mean that getting angry is not being thoughtful.

9. Practice self-reflection.

When things get tough, it's natural to feel irritated by what another person is doing to cause tension. Yet it's important to wonder about our own role as well, asking ourselves questions like these: What am I doing to contribute to creating a barrier or tension? What about me makes me feel this way? How am I presenting my ideas and experience or receiving the ideas and experience of others?

10. Know that it's okay to make mistakes.

We learn by expressing our ideas and getting feedback from others. Mistakes and the expression of misinformation are ways to get new information. Holding back for fear of making those mistakes can mean lost opportunity for growth as well as unfairly leaving the risk-taking responsibility to others.

11. Assume that we all have a desire for knowledge and growth.

We all have a lot to learn—and are always learning. We're not all in the same place. Some of us may have a great deal of knowledge in some areas but not much in others. We can support each other's learning and growth rather than judge or try to "one-up." Remember we were each once, and will be again, the one who hadn't "gotten it" yet.

12. Use "both/and" thinking rather than "either/or" thinking.

Rather than one perspective or solution being the good or right thing and another the bad or wrong thing, allow for more than one simultaneously valid perspective or solution. Exploring two or more perspectives is often more productive than trying to reconcile them.

13. Expect a long-term process.

Dealing with difficult issues can take a long time, with many changes along the way. Many of the same issues will come up over and over.

14. Take responsibility for what's happening.

While the role of facilitator(s) is important to the group, everyone's participation can make a big difference in how well things go. For example, the expertise and experience of the whole group can respond to difficult questions or help keep the discussion on track.

Appendix B

Checklist for Creating and Assessing Anti-Bias Environments

This checklist is an attempt to give practitioners a relatively simplified source to refer to in the ongoing process of implementing an anti-bias approach and reevaluating what works and what still needs attention.

The list is in many ways a work in progress. Feel free to add to it and to make adjustments necessary for cultural relevancy.

1. Staff learn about similarities and differences.

   - Staff make a commitment to and develop a plan for learning about cultural and individual similarities and differences related to the following:

      — Values, such as independence versus interdependence

      — Child-rearing practices

      — Communication and learning styles

      — Expression and resolution of conflict

   - Staff practice negotiating diverse styles of communication and conflict.

2. Staff learn about bias.

   - Staff make a commitment to and develop a plan for learning about their own biases.

      — Read or view and discuss books, articles, and videos about racism, classism, and other biases.

      — Attend relevant training, courses, and workshops.

      — Discuss bias, its sources, and its impact on those to whom it is directed as well as those who carry it.

      — Review and analyze racism, sexism, and other biases in popular media for adults.

      — Analyze bias in language.

      — Collect and discuss scenarios reflecting bias.

      — Practice responding to bias.

3. Staff make a commitment to intervene when bias is expressed by other adults.

- Staff make a commitment to intervention that models questioning and investigation:

  —Indicate refusal to collaborate with bias.

  —Learn more about a person's experience and reasons for the expression of bias.

  —Encourage critical thinking.

- Staff make a commitment to counteract expressions of bias.

  —Avoid generalizations that are stereotypes.

  —Abstain from jokes and put-downs related to bias.

  —Use nonbiased language.

  —Provide information.

  —Protest and organize in various ways.

4. Staff develop implementation strategies for the classroom.

- Staff strategize ways to implement an anti-bias approach.

  —Review and analyze school materials and policies for diversity and bias.

  —Record and discuss other issues related to bias in the workplace.

  —Observe, record, and discuss what children are saying and doing in the program related to diversity and bias.

  —Learn about and discuss what diversity and bias children are being exposed to outside the program through popular media and other sources.

  —Practice responding to bias expressed by children.

5. Staff strategize ways to implement an anti-bias approach.

- Staff involve family members.

  —Hold meetings of families and staff to explore issues of bias and related curriculum strategies.

  —Encourage family members to share information about bias they experience and to tell their stories of confronting it.

  —Invite family members to critique activities, books, and materials for bias relevant to their own experiences with bias.

—Ask family members to be a resource for photographs, music, translations, classroom visitors, or field trips to work sites.

6. Staff implement an anti-bias approach: the classroom.

- Staff assess the learning environment.

  —Recognize and support diverse learning styles in the development of daily plans and activities, while encouraging children to try new ways of interacting with people and materials. Example: Some children come from families where emphasis is put on interdependence. They prefer working with a companion or trusted adult to get started with something new or difficult. Others come from families where the emphasis is more on independence and so are more likely to try things on their own.

- Staff learn what stereotypes and biased attitudes children already hold.

  —Observe, listen, and record children's comments and interactions reflecting bias.

  —Using a variety of photographs, have children talk about the people in them and group the people they think can be friends or family.

- Staff encourage children's awareness of diversity and their positive recognition of diverse perspectives.

  —Introduce children to diverse people through field trips, visitors to class, books, photographs in displays, and dramatic play.

  —Find their similarities and their differences, beginning with differences that are least likely to carry value judgments. (Be careful as you move into areas that do carry value judgments. Know that the acknowledgment of those differences, even your attempts to validate them, will probably lead to some teasing and thus intervention. The teasing will lessen as children learn to challenge negative messages regarding differences.)

  —Experiment with doing the same thing in different ways.

  —Compare perspectives on different events, books, or activities.

  —Read books that illustrate diverse perspectives and ways of doing things.

—Brainstorm a variety of solutions to problems as they arise.

—Point out the variety of methods children use for doing similar things.

• Staff acknowledge bias and teach children to stand up against it.

—Compare stereotypes to reality.

—Use books, puppet plays, family and staff stories, or relevant community struggles to model responding to bias.

—Critique solutions applied in various stories and role-playing, and think about what else could be done to promote cooperative strategies.

—Have children brainstorm what they would do in situations involving bias.

—Have children practice responding to bias by acting out short stories or scenarios using puppets or skits.

—Encourage children to apply the strategies in relevant ways.

—Intervene when children make remarks reflecting bias.

—Follow up after interventions related to bias.

—Regularly reevaluate materials and curriculum for bias related to age, gender, sexual orientation, family composition, class, physical abilities, physical characteristics, race, and ethnicity.

7. Staff implement an anti-bias approach: interactions.

• Staff pay the same attention to, and pick up as quickly on, nonverbal and verbal expressions of interest with:

girls as with boys

children of color as with white children

light-skinned children of color as with dark-skinned children of color

children with diverse physical abilities as with able-bodied children

• Staff interpret and respond in the same way to similar behaviors with:

boys as with girls

children of color as with white children

light-skinned children of color as with dark-skinned children of color able-bodied children as with children with diverse physical abilities

- Staff maintain balance in these ways as well:

  —Girls and boys receive compliments equally on appearance and on achievement.

  —Adapted opportunities are available for children with various physical abilities to interact actively and independently with materials and other children.

  —Caregivers don't overprotect/underprotect children or provide too much/too little help for them because of diverse physical abilities, gender, or race.

  —When children ask or make comments about various physical differences, they receive direct, accurate feedback.

  —When children touch an adult's or child's hair or skin, or make comments about skin color or hair texture, caregivers support and facilitate their explorations instead of ignoring or redirecting them.

  —Caregivers consciously reflect on and reevaluate the messages they send children.

8. Staff implement an anti-bias approach: the visual environment.

   - Staff create an environment that reflects students' lives.

     —Make available a camera and money for film and developing costs to take photographs of children, staff, and families in the program for use in displays, games, and books.

   - Staff create a visual environment that supports diversity using books, photographs, and other displays.

   - Use stereotypic images as tools for teaching about bias.

   - Continually reevaluate images in the environment, including the images in computer programs, packaging of materials, food containers, clothing, play figures, puppets, and puzzles.

   - Staff use the following guidelines for choosing visual images:

     —Include lots of photographs of all the children, families, and staff in the program.

     —Reflect the various backgrounds of each child and the people they live with.

     —Reflect people unlike the children in the class.

—Focus on daily life, not special events and celebrations.

—Focus on the present rather than the past.

—Seek images depicting cooperation, working together, and people helping each other.

—Seek images depicting struggles for justice and human rights.

—Include groups of people who are often absent from school materials based on racism, ethnocentrism, classism, sexism, homophobia, ableism, ageism, and other forms of the dominant cultural bias.

• Staff avoid repeatedly according low status to certain groups and jobs in classroom materials.

—Make sure a wide range of people are illustrated both in positions generally considered to be of high status and in positions generally considered to be of low status.

Examples: Females are shown equally as often in roles such as doctor as well as nurse; people of Afro-Caribbean or Asian origin are shown in roles such as bank manager and head teacher as often as they are in roles such as bus driver and food server.

• Staff avoid "tokenizing" people by repeatedly portraying them as follows:

—Only one of a group

—Peripheral, nonessential roles

—Put on the last page

—Drawn as white people with only a change in skin color, rather than as people with their own individual features

• Staff reflect diverse images of family composition.

—Single-parent families led by men and women

—Extended families

—Families with two mothers or two fathers

—Families in which one parent and a grandparent are the parents

—Families in which a grandparent or grandparents are the parents

—Interracial and multiethnic families

—Adopted and foster families

- Staff reflect images of families that reflect diversity, including:

  — Class

  — Race

  — Ethnicity

  — Age

  — Physical abilities

  — Physical characteristics such as body size or wearing eyeglasses

- Staff provide images of class diversity that are at least 50 percent reflective of the full range of working-class life in order to:

  — Counter the dominant images of middle- and upper-class life

  — Assist economically advantaged children in developing a more realistic understanding and less superior picture of themselves in the world

- Staff provide images of males and females who share the same range of traits and participate in the same range of activities.

  — Nontraditional jobs inside and outside the home

  — Different types of work, including "blue-collar" jobs (factory workers, repair persons), "pink-collar" jobs (beauticians, salespersons), and "white-collar" jobs (teachers, doctors)

  — Displaying behaviors such as:

    making decisions

    leading

    helping

    receiving help

    solving problems

    being active

    crying (or sad)

    observing

    caring for children

- Staff provide images of people with diverse physical characteristics, such as body size or wearing eyeglasses, that include diversity of:

  —Class

  —People doing different kinds of work

  —Race

  —Ethnicity

  —Age

  —Physical abilities

  —Family composition

  —Recreational activities

- Staff provide images of people who are physically challenged. Include diversity of:

  —Class

  —Employment

  —Race

  —Ethnicity

  —Age

  —Physical ability

  —Family composition

  —Recreational activities

- Staff portray people with physical disabilities as productive members of society with emphasis on what they can do rather than on what they can't do.

  —Important family members

  —Students

  —Teachers

  —Workers

- If the population of the class is predominantly children with diverse physical challenges, staff provide extra images of children and adults with diverse physical challenges doing a broad range of activities.

- Staff provide images of elderly men and women that include the following:

- —Involvement in social activities outside the home

- —Involvement in nonstereotypical activities

- —Independent and active behaviors versus dependent and passive behaviors

- —People who are single, widowed, or divorced as well as married

- —Equal numbers of men and women

- —Diverse races and ethnic groups

- —Diverse physical abilities and physical characteristics

- —People from various economic backgrounds doing diverse activities

- —Connections between the young and old

- —Grandparents acting as parents

- —Romantic possibilities between people over sixty years old

- Staff provide images of people of color and nondominant ethnic groups.

  - —Children and adults from the major racial/ethnic groups in the community and in U.S. society

  - —People's current lives rather than their lives in the past or during special holiday celebrations

  - —A numerical balance among different groups

- If the population of the class is predominantly children of color, staff is sure that more than half of the images and materials reflect their backgrounds in order to counter the predominance of white cultural images in the general society.

- If the population of the class is predominantly white children, staff is sure that at least half of the images introduce diversity in order to counter the white-centered images of the dominant culture.

- Staff include images of people not living in the United States that make connections between them and Americans.

  - —Choose global images based on addressing bias rather than simply to increase diversity

  - —People involved in familiar activities such as cooking, eating, playing, working, and recreation

- Staff provide images that depict people in both urban and rural settings. Avoid or challenge stereotypes of rural life as primitive or not as good as urban life by choosing images that depict similarities between urban and rural life.

  —Children playing in similar ways or with similar toys

  —Types of work people do to meet similar needs

  —Children with their families

- Staff provide images of important individuals.

  —Past and present

  —Diversity of race, ethnicity, gender, physical ability, and class background

  —People who participate(d) in important struggles for social justice

  —Everyday heroes: The important people in our communities and families who struggle in the face of oppression or poverty

- Provide images of art.

  —A variety of tans, browns, and blacks in materials such as paint, paper, collage materials, playdough, and crayons

  —Artwork (paintings, drawings, or sculpture) and artists of diverse backgrounds creating their art

  —Prints, sculpture, textiles, and other artwork that reflect the aesthetic environments and cultures of:

    families represented in the classroom

    diverse groups in the community

    diverse groups in the United States

9. Staff implement an anti-bias approach: books.

- Staff choose books that:

  —Reflect the backgrounds of the families in the classroom

  —Reflect the diversity of children and families within a group and, to avoid tokenism, provide more than one book about a particular culture, race, or lifestyle

  —Reflect accurate information and images (not stereotypes) depicting diversity of:

    gender roles

    racial backgrounds

ethnic backgrounds (emphasizing major groups in your community and in the nation)

physical abilities

occupations, including factory workers, repair people, beauticians, salespersons, teachers, and doctors

ages

family composition

use alphabet and story books in different languages, including Braille and sign language

- Staff emphasize stories that show:

  —Cooperation, working together, and people helping each other

  —Daily contemporary lives—working, being with family, problem solving—with less emphasis on celebrations

  —Struggles for justice and human rights

  —Different ways of living and solving similar problems

  —Groups of people that are often absent from school materials because of racism, ethnocentrism, classism, sexism, homophobia, ableism, ageism, and other forms of dominant culturalism

- Staff choose books that avoid "tokenizing" people by repeatedly portraying them as:

  —Only one of a group

  —Peripheral, nonessential

  —Added on the last page

  —Drawn as white people with only a change in skin color, rather than as people with their own individual features

- Staff avoid repeatedly giving low status to certain groups and jobs in classroom materials. Make sure a wide range of people are illustrated both in positions generally considered to be of high status and in positions generally considered to be of low status. Examples:

  —Show females in roles such as doctor as well as nurse.

  —Show people of Afro-Caribbean or Asian origin in roles such as bank managers and head teachers, as well as bus drivers and school dinner helpers.

- Staff continually reevaluate books they are using.

  — Use books with stereotypic images and inaccurate information as tools for teaching about bias or eliminate them from daily use.

  — Select books and stories about other countries that are relevant to the children in the program and that specifically develop respect and challenge stereotypes and dehumanizing images children receive from their environment.

  — Story lines to be avoided: See the examples of story lines provided in many of the chapters.

10. Staff implement an anti-bias approach: dramatic play.

- For diversity of gender play, staff will ensure:

  — Tools and spaces for working in and out of the house

  — House props that can be other than for the kitchen

  — Props, clothing, and spaces that provide a variety of changing dramatic play arenas, such as a factory, hospital, store, mechanic shop, or bakery

  — Dramatic play props are changed periodically to encourage diverse roles

  — Boys and girls encouraged in all areas, with areas rearranged if necessary to do so

  — Time set aside for just boys or just girls to encourage children to play in areas not chosen based on gender

  — A balance of male and female dolls with a variety of clothes allowing for diversity of gender roles

- Beginning with the variation in their own children's homes, staff show things that reflect ethnic diversity.

  — Various cooking and eating objects

  — Various work tools and clothes

  — Personal objects, such as different kinds of combs and brushes

  — Relevant photographs

  — Doll and people accessories, photograph displays, or other items that represent a balance of the major ethnic groups in the United States

- Staff address diverse physical abilities.

  —Make the tools used by people with diverse physical abilities, such as wheelchairs, crutches, braces, canes, eyeglasses, and hearing aids, available for exploration.

  —Create spaces that are navigable by children using wheelchairs or crutches.

  —Provide a selection of dolls, puppets, and play figures with diverse physical abilities reflecting various racial and ethnic backgrounds, as well as males and females of different ages.

- Staff address racial diversity.

  —Provide doll and people accessories, photograph displays, or other items that represent a balance of the major racial groups in the United States, including African Americans, Latinos and Latinas, Asian Americans, Native Americans, and white Americans.

  —Allow for diverse family configurations.

11. Staff implement an anti-bias approach: language.

- The environment should provide numerous opportunities for children to see and hear various languages, including American Sign Language. Begin with any language that children and their families or staff speak and then expand to those found in the community, city, or nation. Look for language used in labeling materials.

  —Alphabet and number posters

  —Story tapes

  —Songs and records

  —Finger plays

  —Food containers for dramatic play

  —Books that include stories addressing issues of bias related to language

12. Staff implement an anti-bias approach: music.

- Staff ensures that regularly heard music reflects the various cultural styles of the children and staff.

  —Singing

  —Background music

—Music for movement

—Music at naptime

- Staff choose other music to reflect various cultural styles beyond those represented in the classroom with emphasis on that of major groups in the United States.

13. Staff implement an anti-bias approach: manipulatives.

- Staff allow for regularly available manipulative materials— puzzles, play people, lotto games, card games—that depict diversity of race, ethnicity, gender, physical ability, occupation, and class.

Sources

Guidelines for selecting bias-free textbooks and storybooks. 1980. New York: Council on Interracial Books for Children.

Derman-Sparks, Louise, and the A.B.C. Task Force. 1989. *Anti-bias curriculum: Tools for empowering young children.* Washington, DC: National Association for the Education of Young Children.

Inner London Education Authority Learning Resources Branch. 1985. *Everyone counts: Looking for bias and insensitivity in primary mathematics materials.* London, England: Inner London Education Authority Learning Resources Branch.

Rigg, Pat, Francis E. Kazemek, and Sarah Hudelson. Spring 1993. Children's books about the elderly. *Rethinking Schools.*

Wolpert, Ellen. 1998. *Strategies for implementing an anti-bias approach in programs for young children.* Unpublished manuscript.

Appendix C

Ten Quick Ways to Analyze Children's Books for Sexism and Racism

Young children are exposed to racist and sexist attitudes both in and out of school. These attitudes, expressed over and over in books and other media, gradually distort their perceptions until stereotypes and myths are accepted as reality. It's difficult to convince children to question society's attitudes. But if a child can be shown how to detect racism and sexism in a book, the child can transfer that perception to wider areas. The following ten guidelines are offered as a starting point to evaluate children's books from this perspective.

1. Check the illustrations.

   - *Look for stereotypes.* Stereotypes are oversimplified generalizations about a particular group, race, or sex, that usually carry derogatory implications. Some infamous, overt stereotypes are the happy-go-lucky, watermelon-eating African American; the sombrero-wearing, fiesta-loving, macho Chicano; the inscrutable, slant-eyed Asian American; the naked, savage, or "primitive" Native American and his "squaw"; the gang member, switchblade-toting Puerto Rican; the completely domesticated woman, the doll-loving little girl, the demure mother, or the wicked stepmother. While you may not always find stereotypes in the blatant forms described, look for variations that in any way demean or ridicule characters because of their race or sex.

   - *Look for tokenism.* If there are characters of color in the illustrations, do they look just like whites except for being tinted or colored in? Do all faces of people of color look alike, or are they depicted as genuine individuals with distinctive features?

   - *Who's doing what?* Do the illustrations depict people of color in subservient and passive roles, or in leadership and action roles? Are males the active "doers" and females the inactive observers?

2. Check the story line.

- The liberation movements have led publishers to weed out many insulting passages, particularly from stories with black themes and from books depicting female characters. However, racist and sexist attitudes still find expression in less obvious ways. The following checklist suggests some of the subtle, covert forms of bias to watch for.

    — *Standard for success.* Does it take "white" behavior standards for a person of color to "get ahead"? Is "making it" in the dominant white society projected as the only ideal? To gain acceptance and approval, does the person who is the target of bias have to exhibit extraordinary qualities (excel in sports, get As in school)? In friendships between white children and children of color, is it the child of color who does most of the understanding and forgiving?

    — *Resolution of problems.* How are problems presented, conceived, and resolved in the story? Are people of color considered to be "the problem"? Are the oppressions faced by people of color and women represented as causally related to an unjust society? Are the reasons for poverty and oppression explained, or are they accepted as inevitable? Does the story line encourage passive acceptance or active resistance? Is a particular problem that a person of color faces resolved through the benevolent intervention of a white person?

    — *Role of women.* Are the achievements of girls and women based on their own initiative and intelligence? Or are they due to their good looks or to their relationship with boys? Are sex roles incidental or critical to characterization and plot? Could the same story be told if the sex roles were reversed?

3. Look at the lifestyles.

- Are people of color and their settings depicted in such a way that they contrast unfavorably with the unstated norm of white, middle-class suburbia? If the group in question is depicted as "different," are negative value judgments implied? Are people of color depicted exclusively in ghettos, barrios, or migrant camps? If the illustrations and text attempt to depict another culture, do they go beyond oversimplifications and offer genuine insights into another lifestyle? Look for inaccuracy and inappropriateness in the depiction of other cultures. Watch for instances of the "quaint natives in costume" syndrome (most noticeable in areas like clothing and custom, but extending to behavior and personality traits as well).

4. Weigh the relationships between people.

- Do the whites in the story possess the power, take the leadership, and make the important decisions? Do people of color and females function in essentially supporting, subservient roles?

- How are family relationships depicted? In black families, is the mother always dominant? In Latino families, are there always lots of children? If the family is separated, are societal conditions (unemployment, poverty) cited among the reasons for the separation?

5. Note the heroes.

- For many years, books showed only "safe" heroes of color—those who avoided serious conflict with the white establishment of their time. People of color today are insisting on the right to define their own heroes (of both sexes) based on their own concepts and struggles for justice.

- When heroes of color do appear, are they admired for the same qualities that have made white heroes famous or because what they have done has benefited white people? Ask the question "Whose interest is this hero really serving?" That of the hero's own people? Or that of white people?

6. Consider the effects on a child's self-image.

- Are norms established that limit any child's aspirations and conceptions of self? What effect can it have on children of color to be continuously bombarded with images of the color white as the ultimate in beauty, cleanliness, and virtue while the color black is evil, dirty, or menacing? Does the book reinforce or counteract positive associations with the color white and negative associations with the color black?

- What happens to a girl's self-image when she reads that boys perform all of the brave and important deeds? What about a girl's self-esteem if she is not "fair" of skin and slim of body?

- In a particular story, is there one or more persons with whom a child of color can readily identify to a positive and constructive end?

7. Consider the author's or illustrator's background.

- Analyze the biographical material on the jacket flap or the back of the book. If a story deals with a theme involving people of color, what qualifies the author or illustrator to deal with the subject? If the author and illustrator are not members of the group being written about, is there anything in their background that would specifically recommend them as the creators of this book?

8. Check out the author's perspective.

- No author can be entirely objective. All authors write from a cultural context as well as from a personal one. In the past, children's books have traditionally come from authors who were white and middle class, with a single ethnocentric perspective dominating. With any book in question, read carefully to determine whether the direction of the author's perspective substantially weakens or strengthens the value of the written work. Is the perspective patriarchal or feminist? Is it solely Eurocentric, or do third-world perspectives also surface?

9. Watch for loaded words.

- A "loaded" word has offensive overtones. Examples of loaded adjectives (usually racist) are savage, primitive, conniving, lazy, superstitious, treacherous, wily, crafty, inscrutable, docile, and backward.

- Look for sexist language and adjectives that exclude or in any way demean girls or women. Look for use of the male pronoun to refer to both males and females. While the generic use of the word man was accepted in the past, its use today is outmoded. The following examples show how sexist language can be avoided by using gender-neutral terms:

Biased Term	Gender-Neutral Term
forefathers	ancestors
chairman	chairperson
brotherhood	community
firemen	firefighters
man-made	manufactured
the family of man	the human family

10. Look at the copyright date.

- Books on people of color—usually hastily conceived—suddenly began appearing in the mid- and late-1960s. There followed a growing number of "minority experience" books to meet the new market demand, but these books were still written by white authors, edited by white editors, and published by white publishers. They therefore reflected a white point of view. Not until the early 1970s did the children's book world begin to even remotely reflect the realities of a pluralistic society. Copyright dates can therefore be a clue as to how likely the book is to be overtly racist or sexist, although a recent copyright date, of course, is no guarantee of a book's relevance or sensitivity. The copyright date only tells the year the book was published. It usually takes two years—and often much more than that—from the time a manuscript is submitted to the publisher to the time it is actually printed and put on the market. This time lag meant little in the past, but in a period of rapid change and new consciousness, when children's book publishing is attempting to be "relevant," the lag is becoming increasingly significant.

Source

Adapted from the Council on Interracial Books for Children, New York.

Appendix D

Photograph Games for an Anti-Bias Approach

Tools

- **Clear Con-Tact paper** to cover pictures after they are mounted on mat board. Order clear Con-Tact paper from educational catalogs, or purchase it by the roll at local hardware stores.

- **Mat board** to mount pictures on. Picture-framing businesses will often give away mat board scraps for free. It can also be purchased but is relatively expensive. Other stiff cardboard or oak tag can be used. Mat board's advantage is that it does not bend easily.

- **Paper cutter** to cut the mat board. If you purchase or obtain fairly large-size mat board, it is best to have a paper cutter that is at least as large as your boards. The smaller cutters—18 or 12 inches—are easier to handle if you are working with smaller pieces. I recommend establishing standard sizes and cutting all your game boards to these sizes. This facilitates sorting pictures into different themes for a variety of games. I recommend using 5- by-7-inch cards. Pictures too large for this size can be made into puzzles.

- **Double-sided tape** to attach pictures to the mat board.

- **Scissors** to cut Con-Tact paper to size if you don't use the paper cutter and to cut in at the corners to avoid overlap as you fold the contact paper over the boards.

- **Marking pens.** I recommend fine- and extra-fine-point Sharpie permanent markers.

Suggestions for Preparing Game Boards

- Keep an ongoing collection of pictures. When cutting them out, write down information about the picture, or cut out the information and keep it with the picture. A need for it may arise later. Sort the pictures by category, game type, or size, and keep them in files.

- Cut the mat board into standard sizes.

- Place pictures on the mat board using the double-sided tape. Place the pictures near the bottom or top of the board and leave room for labels you may want to attach now or later.

- Cut Con-Tact paper about 1½ inches larger all the way around than the mat board you are covering.

- Use a work surface that the Con-Tact paper won't stick to.

- Peel contact paper and place it sticky-side-up on your work surface.

- Place the mat board, with the picture on it, facedown in the center of the Con-Tact paper.

- Cut the Con-Tact paper from the corners. Pull away the corners. (Cutting this way will prevent the Con-Tact paper from overlapping on itself.)

- Turn the board and Con-Tact paper sticky-side-down. Starting from the center of the picture, carefully rub toward the edge to remove any air bubbles.

- Tightly fold up the edges of the Con-Tact paper.

Suggested Sources of Photographs

Note that some of these books are out of print but are typically available through online booksellers and bookstores that sell out-of-print and used books.

- *The African Americans: A Celebration of Achievement,* edited by Charles M. Collins and David Cohen (New York: Penguin, 1995).

- *Children of Asian America,* compiled by Gene H. Mayeda on behalf of the Asian American Coalition (Chicago: Polychrome Publishing, 1995).

- *Family: A Portrait of Gay and Lesbian America,* by Nancy Andrews (San Francisco: HarperSanFrancisco, 1994). Photographs showing young and old people, as well as white people and people of color, including African Americans, Latinos, and Asians. Some of the photographs show families with children, some show couples, and others are of individuals.

- *Family Portraits in Changing Times,* by Helen Nestor (Salt Lake City: New Sage Press, 1992). This book has an excellent collection of photographs of diverse families. I recommend buying more than one copy—use one for making games and keep the other copy to look at and talk about.

- *Fathers and Sons: Photographs,* by Steven Begleiter (New York: Abbeville, 1989). A collection of photographs of fathers and their sons. Some of the photographs show young children and others are of adult children and their fathers; some include three generations—from grandfather to grandson.

- *Generations: A Universal Family Album,* edited by Anna R. Cohn and Lucinda A. Leach with an introduction by Sheila Kitzinger (New York: Pantheon Books, 1987). This book has many wonderful photographs of men and women with children.

- *In America,* by Eve Arnold (New York: Knopf, 1983). A very diverse collection of photographs from the United States.

- *National Geographic.* Often these magazines are available cheaply from bookstores and thrift shops selling used books. Note, however, that many of the articles portray "exotic" groups within a country. You will need to search for several articles about a particular country. Look for both urban and rural settings. Focus on daily activities that have something in common with the lives of the children in your program, and avoid special ceremonies and holidays.

- *Navajo: Portrait of a Nation,* by Joel Grimes (Englewood, CO: Westcliffe, 1992).

- *Organizing for Our Lives: New Voices from Rural Communities,* by Richard Steven Street (Salt Lake City: New Sage Press, 1993).

- *Songs of My People: African-Americans, A Self-Portrait,* edited by Eric Easter (New York: Little, Brown, 1992). An excellent collection of photographs of African Americans.

- *Vision Quest: Men, Women, and Sacred Sites of the Sioux Nation,* with photographs by Don Doll (New York: Crown, 1994).

- *Women and Work: Photographs and Personal Writings,* edited by Maureen R. Michelson and Michael R. Dressler (Salt Lake City: New Sage Press, 1986). An extensive collection of photographs showing women in diverse work situations. The book does an excellent job of portraying white women in nontraditional jobs. There are a number of excellent photographs of women of color. Note, however, that there are a few too many photographs of African American women in stereotypical housekeeping roles. To provide a stronger collection of images, search for additional books that show women of color at work in nonstereotypical jobs.

- Children's books. Children's photographic essay books are excellent sources of pictures. Story books are often illustrated with diverse art styles and depict diverse people in nonstereotypical roles. If you don't want to cut up books that are in good condition, you can wait until they are well used and beginning to fall apart.

- Magazines. Plenty of images, but note that many magazines rely heavily on images of middle-class people and people who have been carefully dressed and made up. They generally don't reflect the majority of people in this nation involved in a wide range of daily activities, dressed as they would be for those activities, nor do they show a wide range of natural skin color and type, hairstyles, and body sizes.

Appendix E

Guidelines for Challenging Racism and Other Forms of Oppression

1. Challenge discriminatory attitudes and behavior! Ignoring the issues will not make them go away. Silence can send the message that you agree with such attitudes and behaviors. Make it clear that you will not tolerate racial, ethnic, religious, or sexual jokes or slurs, or any actions that demean any person or group. Your intervention may not always take place at the exact time or place of the incident, but the incident must be addressed promptly.

2. Expect tension and conflict and learn to manage it. Sensitive and deep-seated issues are unlikely to change without some struggle. In many situations, conflict is unavoidable. Face your fears and discomforts and remember that tension and conflict can be positive forces that foster growth.

3. Be aware of your own attitudes, stereotypes, and expectations. Be open to discovering the limitations they place on your perspective. We have all been socialized to believe many myths and misconceptions. None of us remain untouched by the discriminatory messages in our society. Be honest with yourself about your own prejudices and biases, and practice not getting defensive when they are pointed out to you. If you don't know something, or aren't sure how to handle a situation, say so, then seek the information or help that you need.

4. Actively listen to and learn from others' experiences. Don't minimize, trivialize, or deny people's concerns. Make an effort to see situations through their eyes.

5. Use language and behavior that are nonbiased. Use language that is inclusive of all people regardless of race, ethnicity, sex, disability, sexual orientation, class, age, and religion.

6. Provide accurate information to challenge stereotypes and biases. Take responsibility for educating yourself about your own culture and that of others. Don't expect people from different backgrounds to always educate you about their culture or history, or to explain racism or sexism to you. People are

more willing to share when you take an active role and when the learning is mutual.

7. Acknowledge diversity and avoid stereotypical thinking. Don't ignore or pretend not to see our rich human differences. Acknowledging obvious differences isn't the problem—placing negative value judgments on those differences is! Stereotypes about those differences are always hurtful because they generalize, limit, and deny people's full humanity.

8. Be aware of your own hesitancies to intervene in these kinds of situations. Confront your own fears about interrupting discrimination, set your priorities, and take action. Develop "response-ability"!

9. Project a feeling of understanding, love, and support when confronting individuals. Without preaching, state how you feel and firmly address the hurtful behavior or attitude while supporting the dignity of the person. Be nonjudgmental, but know the bottom line. Issues of human dignity, justice, and safety are nonnegotiable.

10. Establish standards of responsibility and behavior. Hold yourself and others accountable. Demonstrate your personal and organizational commitment in practices, policies, and procedures, both formal and informal. Maintain high expectations for all people.

11. Be a role model willing to take the risks that leadership demands. Reflect and practice anti-bias and multicultural values in all aspects of your life. Demonstrate that you respect and value the knowledge, talents, and diversity of all people.

12. Work collectively with others. Organize and support efforts that combat prejudice and oppression in all its forms. Social change is a long-term struggle. It's easy to get discouraged, but together we have the strength and vision to make a difference.

Source

Patti DeRosa, President, ChangeWorks Consulting (formerly Cross-cultural Consultation), 28 S. Main St. #113, Randolph, MA 02368; Web site: www.changeworksconsulting.org.

Appendix F

Practice Responding to Bias

For practice responding to incidents involving bias, use the individual scenarios presented in each chapter, or keep a log of other examples from your own settings. Use the following questions adapted from Margie Carter and Deb Curtis's (1994) book *Training Teachers: A Harvest of Theory and Practice* and from *Learning to Listen, Learning to Teach* by Jane Vella (1994).

1. What happened? Consider the following:

   - What issues of bias are involved?

   - What is your bias in this situation?

   - How does the situation make you feel?

   - Is there conflict between your own beliefs and those of other adults involved or those of the families of the children involved?

2. Why did it happen? Consider the following:

   - Why do the people involved have the ideas they have?

   - What societal images and messages are influencing them?

3. What's the impact of what happened? Consider the following:

   - The impact on people directly involved.

   - The impact on others who overhear.

4. What intervention can change what happened? Consider the following:

   - What do you want to accomplish?

   - If there is conflict between your own beliefs and those of other adults or the families of children involved, how will you be respectful of those beliefs?

   - What developmental issues will influence your response?

   - What can be said to affirm the feelings and identity of each person?

   - What questions will model investigation and encourage critical thinking rather than interrogation that will embarrass or shame?

- What questions will encourage children to reflect on their own experiences and on new information that you provide?

- What relevant new information is appropriate to provide?

- How can common understandings of fairness be built upon?

- Have you established a safety rule *with* children that you can refer to and if necessary add to?

- What model for activism may be relevant?

- What will empower the victim of this bias?

- If there is conflict, what can be done to help children resolve any part that has nothing to do with bias?

For information about handling conflict with adults, consult Margie Carter and Deb Curtis (1994) in *Training Teachers: A Harvest of Theory and Practice*. They build on an approach from Jean Illsely Clark's (1989) book, *Growing Up Again: How to Parent Yourself So You Can Parent Your Children*, which involves seven choices of how to respond to any given conflict. This is helpful material to review in addressing incidents involving bias. The seven choices they identify are attack, defend, empathize, investigate, reframe, excuse, and ignore.

Practice using the seven choices with sample scenarios like the one below from *Training Teachers*. As you practice, consider what you want to accomplish and which response would most likely achieve it.

- Sample scenario: A father comes to pick up his child and finds him in the housekeeping area, dressed in girls' clothing and feeding a baby. The father is clearly upset and comes to you saying he wants his son kept away from "that kind of play."

- Choice of Responses:

  —Attack: We let children play wherever they want; why don't you?

  —Defend: There's no way I could stop your child from playing dress-up.

  —Empathize: It's hard to see your child doing something you disapprove of.

  —Investigate: Are you worried that he might get teased or picked on?

  —Reframe: I'd like to understand what harm you think this might do to your child. From what I know, young children who are prevented from exploring their interests and identity in a supervised environment often grow up with confusion—if not shame—about who they are.

— Excuse: Oh, don't worry; it's just harmless play.

— Ignore: Excuse me; I'm needed out on the playground.

Sources

Carter, Margie, and Deb Curtis. 1994. *Training teachers: A harvest of theory and practice*. St. Paul: Redleaf Press.

Clark, Jane Illsely. 1989. *Growing up again: How to parent yourself so you can parent your children*. New York: Harper.

Vella, Jane. 1994. *Learning to listen, learning to teach*. San Francisco: Jossey-Bass.

Appendix G

Resources for an Anti-Bias Approach

Books and Articles for Adults

This bibliography begins with books and articles that address the general topics of multicultural and anti-bias child care and related issues and then moves on to listings of books that focus on particular issues. The list is in many ways a work in progress; there are issues that are unrepresented or underrepresented. While some books listed may be out of print, they will often still be available from libraries or from bookstores and online booksellers that sell used and out-of-print books.

General Books

Anti-Bias Curriculum: Tools for Empowering Young Children, by Louise Derman-Sparks and the A.B.C. Task Force (Washington, DC: National Association for the Education of Young Children [NAEYC], 1989).

Affirming Diversity: The Sociopolitical Context of Multicultural Education, 4th ed., by Sonia Nieto (New York: Allyn & Bacon, 2003).

Alike and Different: Exploring Our Humanity with Young Children, rev. ed., edited by Bonnie Neugebauer (Washington, DC: NAEYC, 1992).

"Approaches to Multicultural Curriculum Reform," by James A. Banks (*Multicultural Leader* 1 [2], Spring 1988).

The Brown Papers: An occasionally published essay of reflection and analysis from the Women's Theological Center (WTC), P. O. Box 1200, Boston, MA 02117; telephone 617-585-5655; Web site www.thewtc.org.

Common Bonds: Anti-Bias Teaching in a Diverse Society, 2nd ed., edited by Deborah A. Byrnes and Gary Kiger (Wheaton, MD: Association for Childhood Education International, 1996).

Cultural Etiquette: A Guide for the Well-Intentioned, by Amoja Three Rivers (Indian Valley, VA: Market Wimmin, 1991). Market Wimmin's address is Box 28, Indian Valley, VA 24105.

Culture and Power in the Classroom: A Critical Foundation for Bicultural Education, by Antonia Darder (Westport, CT: Greenwood, 1991).

Deepening Our Understanding of Anti-Bias Education for Children: An Anthology of Readings, edited by Louise Derman-Sparks and Dorothy Granger (Pasadena, CA: Pacific Oaks College).

Developing Cross-Cultural Competence: A Guide for Working with Children and Their Families, 3rd ed., edited by Eleanor W. Lynch and Marci J. Hanson (Baltimore: Paul H. Brookes Publishing, 2004).

Diversity and Developmentally Appropriate Practices in Early Childhood Education: Challenges for Early Childhood Education, by Bruce L. Mallory and Rebecca S. New (New York: Teachers College Press, 1993).

Diversity in the Classroom: New Approaches to the Education of Young Children, by Frances E. Kendall (New York: Teachers College Press, 1996).

Dumbing Us Down: The Hidden Curriculum of Compulsory Schooling, by John Taylor Gatto (Branford, CT: New Society Publishers, 1991).

Empowerment through Multicultural Education: From Reproduction to Contestation of Social Inequality through Schooling, edited by Christine E. Sleeter (Albany: State University of New York Press, 1990).

Everyone Counts: Looking for Bias and Insensitivity in Primary Mathematics Materials (London: Inner London Education Authority). I purchased this from Development Education Centre, now called TIDE (Teachers in Development Education) Birmingham, Millennium Point, GO4 Curzon Street, Birmingham B4 7XG; Web site: www.tidec.org. Although directed at mathematics materials, this book is applicable to assessing any materials from an anti-bias focus.

Everyone's Kids' Books: A Guide to Multicultural, Socially Conscious Books for Children, by Nancy Braus and Molly Geider (Brattleboro, VT: Everyone's Books, 2000). This guide strives to list books that teach creative, peaceful conflict resolution; help kids appreciate the value of diversity; are set in all sorts of homes, neighborhoods, and cultures; have nonsexist language and messages; and help kids feel empowered and motivated to build a more just world.

Freedom's Plow: Teaching in the Multicultural Classroom, edited by Theresa Perry and James W. Fraser (New York: Routledge, 1993).

Future Vision, Present Work: Learning from the Culturally Relevant Anti-Bias Leadership Project, by Sharon Cronin et al. (St. Paul: Redleaf Press, 1998).

In Our Own Way: How Anti-Bias Work Shapes Our Lives, by Cecelia Alvarado et al. (St. Paul: Redleaf Press, 1999).

Kids Like Us: Using Persona Dolls in the Classroom, by Trisha Whitney (St. Paul: Redleaf Press, 1999).

Literacies of Power: What Americans Are Not Allowed to Know, by Donaldo P. Macedo (Boulder, CO: Westview Press, 1994).

An Introduction to Multicultural Education, 3rd ed., by James A. Banks (New York: Allyn & Bacon, 2001).

"Meeting the Challenge of Diversity," by Elizabeth Jones and Louise Derman-Sparks (*Young Children,* January 1992).

Multicultural Education: Issues and Perspectives, 5th ed., edited by James A. Banks and Cherry A. Banks (Hoboken, NJ: Wiley, 2004).

Multicultural Issues in Child Care, by Janet Gonzalez-Mena (Mountainview, CA: Mayfield Publishing, 1996).

Multiethnic Education: Theory and Practice, 3rd ed., by James A. Banks (Boston: Allyn & Bacon, 1994).

Open Minds to Equality: A Sourcebook of Learning Activities to Affirm Diversity and Promote Equity, 2nd ed., by Nancy Schniedewind and Ellen Davidson (New York: Allyn & Bacon, 1997).

Outlaw Culture: Resisting Representations, by bell hooks (New York: Routledge, 1994).

A Pedagogy for Liberation: Dialogues on Transforming Education, by Ira Shor and Paulo Freire (Westport, CT: Greenwood, 1986).

Racism and Sexism: An Integrated Study, by Paula S. Rothenberg (New York: St. Martin's Press, 1988).

Rethinking Columbus: The Next Five Hundred Years, edited by Bill Bigelow and Bob Peterson (Milwaukee: Rethinking Schools, 1998).

Rethinking Our Classrooms: Teaching for Equity and Justice, by Bill Bigelow (Milwaukee: Rethinking Schools, 1994).

Rethinking Schools: An Urban Educational Journal, 1001 E. Keefe Avenue, Milwaukee, Wisconsin 53212; telephone 414-964-9646.

Rethinking Schools: An Agenda for Change, edited by David Levine et al. (New York: The New Press, 1995).

Roots and Wings: Affirming Culture in Early Childhood Programs, rev. ed., and *Developing Roots and Wings: A Trainer's Guide to Affirming Culture in Early Childhood Programs,* by Stacey York (St. Paul: Redleaf Press, 2003 and 1992).

Savage Inequalities: Children in America's Schools, by Jonathan Kozol (New York: HarperCollins, 1992).

Teaching and Learning in a Diverse World: Multicultural Education for Young Children, 2nd ed., by Patricia Ramsey (New York: Teachers College Press, 1998).

Teaching to Transgress: Education as the Practice of Freedom, by bell hooks (New York: Routledge, 1994).

Teaching Young Children in Violent Times: Building a Peaceable Classroom, 2nd ed., by Diane Levin (Gabriola Island, BC: New Society Publishers, 2003).

Valuing Diversity: The Primary Years, by Janet Brown McCracken (Washington, DC: NAEYC, 1993).

Who's Calling the Shots: How to Respond Effectively to Children's Fascination with War Play and War Toys, by Nancy Carlsson-Paige and Diane Levin (Branford, CT: New Society Publishers, 1990).

African American Issues

Black and White Styles in Conflict, by Thomas Kochman (Chicago: University of Chicago Press, 1995).

Black Children: Their Roots, Culture, and Learning Styles, by Janice E. Hale-Benson (Baltimore: Johns Hopkins University Press, 1986).

Black History for Beginners, by Denise Denis and Susan Willmarth (New York: Writers and Readers Publishing, 1984).

Don't Believe the Hype: Fighting Cultural Misinformation about African Americans, by Farai Chideya (New York: Plume, 1995).

The Dreamkeepers: Successful Teachers of African American Children, by Gloria Ladson-Billings (San Francisco: Jossey-Bass, 1997).

The Maroon within Us: Selected Essays on African American Community Socialization, by Asa G. Hilliard III (Baltimore: Black Classic Press, 1994).

Unbank the Fire: Visions for the Education of African American Children, by Janice E. Hale (Baltimore: Johns Hopkins University Press, 1994).

Age

"Ageism in Children's Books" (*CIBC Bulletin,* Volume 7, numbers 6 and 8, 1976).

"Children's Books about the Elderly," by Pat Rigg, Frances E. Kazemek, and Sarah Hudelson (*Rethinking Schools,* Spring 1993).

Analyzing Media and Literature

The Empire's Old Clothes: What The Lone Ranger, Babar, and Other Innocent Heroes Do to Our Minds, by Ariel Dorfman (New York: Viking Penguin, 1996).

Get the Picture! Developing Visual Literacy in the Infant (Preschool) Classroom (Birmingham, England: Development Education Centre [DEC], 1989). DEC is now called TIDE (Teachers in Development Education) Birmingham, and can be reached at Millennium Point, GO4 Curzon Street, Birmingham B4 7XG; Web site: www.tidec.org.

Guidelines for Selecting Bias-Free Textbooks and Storybooks (New York: Council on Interracial Books for Children [CIBC], 1980). CIBC no longer exists, but the book is available through bookstores and online booksellers that sell used and out-of-print books and from some libraries.

How to Tell the Difference: A Guide to Evaluating Children's Books for Anti-Indian Bias, by Beverly Slapin et al. (Berkeley: Oyate, 1995). Oyate, a Native organization, can be reached at 2702 Mathews St., Berkeley, CA 94702; Web site: www.oyate.org.

"Intolerance is the real message of *The Lion King,*" by Carolyn Newberger (*The Boston Globe,* June 27, 1994).

Should We Burn Babar? Essays on Children's Literature and the Power of Stories, by Herbert Kohl (New York: The New Press, 1995).

Arab Issues

"The Influence of the Arab Stereotype on Children," by Jack Shaheen (Washington, DC: American-Arab Anti-Discrimination Committee Research Institute, 1980). Available from 4201 Connecticut Ave., NW, Suite 300, Washington, DC 20008; telephone 202-244-2990. "Lesson Plan: Anti-Arab Stereotypes, Discrimination, and Hate Crimes," article available for downloading (listed as "Lesson Plan on Stereotypes") from the Web site of the American-Arab Anti-Discrimination Committee: www.adc.org. Click on "education" on the sidebar.

Asian Issues

Children of Asian America, compiled by Gene H. Mayeda on behalf of the Asian American Coalition (Chicago: Polychrome Publishing, 1995).

Chinese Pioneers/Mga Tagapangunang Intsik, by Annie Ching (Berkeley, CA: Asian American Bilingual Center, 1981). Covers the history of Chinese workers in the United States and the discrimination they faced. Although the book is written for children, I have found it useful in introducing adults to aspects of U.S. history that involve the treatment of Chinese immigrants.

The Portrayal of Asian Americans in Children's Books (New York: Council on Interracial Books for Children [CIBC], 1976). CIBC no longer exists, but many of its publications are available in local libraries.

Unlearning Asian American Stereotypes: A Filmstrip and Discussion Guide for Grades 4–9 (New York: Council on Interracial Books for Children [CIBC], 1982). CIBC no longer exists, but many of its publications are available in local libraries.

Body Image

"Respecting Body Size," by Trisha Whitney (*CAEYC* [California Association for the Education of Young Children] *Bulletin,* 30 [1], Fall 1994).

Cooperative Learning

Cooperative Learning, Cooperative Lives: A Sourcebook of Learning Activities for Building a Peaceful World, by Nancy Schniedewind and Ellen Davidson (Dubuque, IA: William C. Brown Company, 1987).

The Cooperative Sports and Games Book: Challenge without Competition, by Terry Orlick (New York: Pantheon Books, 1978).

No Contest: The Case against Competition, rev. ed., by Alfie Kohn (New York: Houghton Mifflin Company, 1992).

Gender Issues

Homophobia: A Weapon of Sexism, expanded ed., by Suzanne Pharr (Inverness, CA: Chardon Press, 1997).

Race, Class, and Gender in the United States: An Integrated Study, 6th ed., by Paula S. Rothenberg (New York: Worth Publishers, 2004).

This Bridge Called My Back: Writings by Radical Women of Color, 3rd ed., edited by Cherríe Moraga and Gloria Anzaldúa (Berkeley, CA: Third Woman Press, 2001).

History

A Different Mirror: A History of Multicultural America, by Ronald Takaki (Boston: Little, Brown, 1994).

Lies My Teacher Told Me: Everything Your American History Textbook Got Wrong, by James W. Loewen (New York: Simon and Schuster, 1996).

A People's History of the United States, rev. ed., by Howard Zinn (New York: HarperCollins, 2003).

Latino and Caribbean Issues

Caribbean Connections—Puerto Rico: Classroom Resources for Secondary Schools, edited by Deborah Menkhart and Catherine A. Sunshine (Washington, DC: Network of Educators on the Americas, 1990).

500 Years of Chicano History in Pictures/500 Años del Pueblo Chicano, edited by Elizabeth Martinez (Albuquerque, NM: Chicano Communications Center, 1991). *Viva La Causa* is a video based on the book.

Palante: Young Lords Party, photographs by Michael Abramson, text by the Young Lords Party and Michael Abramson (New York: McGraw-Hill, 1971).

Teaching about Haiti (Washington, DC: Network of Educators on the Americas, 1993). This book is available from Teaching for Change (formerly Network of Educators on the Americas), P. O. Box 73038, Washington, DC 20056; telephone 800-763-9131; Web site: www.teachingforchange.org.

Unlearning Chicano and Puerto Rican Stereotypes: A Filmstrip and Discussion Guide (New York: Council on Interracial Books for Children [CIBC], 1982). CIBC no longer exists, but many of its publications are available in local libraries.

Native People Issues

Chronicles of American Indian Protest, rev. ed., compiled and edited by the Council on Interracial Books for Children (Greenwich, CT: Fawcett Publications, 1979).

"Columbus and the Quincentennial Myths: Another Side of the Story," by Phyllis Brady (*Young Children,* September 1992).

"The Native American Curriculum: Attempting Alternatives to Tepees and Headbands," by Jane Billman (*Young Children,* September 1992).

"Teaching about Native Americans? Or Teaching about People, Including Native Americans?" by Polly Greenberg (*Young Children,* September 1992).

Unlearning "Indian" Stereotypes: A Teaching Unit for Elementary Teachers and Children's Librarians (New York: The Racism and Sexism Resource Center for Educators, a division of the Council on Interracial Books for Children [CIBC], 1977). CIBC no longer exists, but many of its publications are available in local libraries.

"Wanting to Be Indian: When Spiritual Searching Turns into Cultural Theft," by Myke Johnson, *The Brown Papers,* Boston, April 1995.

"Working with Native American Children," by Lee Little Soldier (*Young Children,* September 1992).

Race and Racism

The Brown Papers: An occasionally published essay of reflection and analysis from the Women's Theological Center (WTC), P. O. Box 1200, Boston, MA 02117; telephone 617-585-5655; Web site www.thewtc.org.

- "The Abolition of Whiteness," by Norene Carter (2 [1], October 1995).

- "The Spiritual Drain of Racism," by Traci C. West (2 [4], January 1996).

- "Who Claims the Label of Victim and Why?" by Ana Ortiz (February 1996).

- "Why We Need a New Abolitionist Movement," by Ann Withorn (1 [10], August–September 1995).

Civil Wars, by June Jordan (New York: Simon & Schuster, 1995).

Crossing the Color Line: Race, Parenting, and Culture, by Maureen T. Reddy (Piscataway, NJ: Rutgers University Press, 1996).

Different and Wonderful: Raising Black Children in a Race-Conscious Society, by Darlene Powell Hopson and Derek S. Hopson (New York: Simon & Schuster, 1992).

The Education of a WASP, by Lois Mark Stalvey (Madison: University of Wisconsin Press, 1989).

Ethnic Identity: The Transformation of White America, by Richard Alba (New Haven, CT: Yale University Press, 1992).

Everyday Acts against Racism: Raising Children in a Multiracial World, edited by Maureen T. Reddy (Seattle: Seal Press, 1996).

Everyday Racism: Reports from Women of Two Cultures, by Philomena Essed (Alameda, CA: Hunter House, 1991).

40 Ways to Raise a Nonracist Child, by Barbara Mathias and Mary Ann French (New York: HarperCollins, 1996).

The Future of the Race, by Henry Louis Gates Jr. and Cornel West (New York: Random House, 1995).

"Historical Reconstruction of the Concept of Race," by James Banks (*Educational Researcher*, March 1995).

Jews and Blacks: A Dialogue on Race, Religion, and Culture in America, by Michael Lerner and Cornel West (New York: Plume, 1996).

Killers of the Dream, by Lillian Smith (New York: W. W. Norton & Company, 1994).

Killing Rage: Ending Racism, by bell hooks (New York: Henry Holt and Company, 1995).

Kwanzaa and Me: A Teacher's Story, by Vivian Gussin Paley (Cambridge, MA: Harvard University Press, 1996).

Letters to Marcia: A Teacher's Guide to Anti-Racist Education, by Enid Lee (Toronto: Cross Cultural Communication Centre, 1985).

Names We Call Home: Autobiography on Racial Identity, edited by Becky Thompson and Sangeeta Tyagi (New York: Routledge, 1996).

Never Say Nigger Again! An Antiracism Guide for White Liberals, by M. Garlinda Burton (Nashville: Winston-Derek Publishers, 1994).

Off White: Readings on Society, Race, and Culture, by Michelle Fine et al. (New York: Routledge, 1996).

On Call: Political Essays, by June Jordan (Cambridge, MA: South End Press, 1985).

Other People's Children: Cultural Conflict in the Classroom, by Lisa Delpit (New York: The New Press, 1996).

Race, Identity, and Representation in Education, edited by Cameron McCarthy and Warren Crichlow (New York: Routledge, 1993). There are some very interesting and important articles in this collection, but many are difficult to read.

A Race Is a Nice Thing to Have: A Guide to Being a White Person or Understanding the White Persons in Your Life, by Janet E. Helms (Topeka, KS: Content Communications, 1992).

Race Matters, by Cornel West (New York: Random, 1994).

Race Traitor, edited by Noel Ignatiev and John Garvey (New York: Routledge, 1996).

Racism 101, by Nikki Giovanni (New York: William Morrow, 1995).

"Role of Whites in Multicultural Education," by James Banks (*Phi Delta Kappan,* September 1993).

Roots of Racism (London: Institute of Race Relations, 1982).

Skin Deep: Black Women and White Women Write about Race, edited by Marita Golden and Susan R. Shreve (New York: Doubleday, 1996).

"Talking about Race, Learning about Racism: The Application of Racial Identity Development Theory in the Classroom," by Beverly Daniel Tatum (*Harvard Educational Review,* 62 [1], Spring 1992).

Teaching/Learning Anti-Racism: A Developmental Approach, by Louise Derman-Sparks and Carol Brunson Phillips (New York: Teachers College Press, 1997).

Technical Difficulties: African-American Notes on the State of the Union, by June Jordan (New York: Vintage Books, 1994).

Through Students' Eyes: Combating Racism in United States Schools, by Karen B. McLean-Donaldson (Westport, CT: Greenwood, 1996).

Towards the Abolition of Whiteness: Essays on Race, Politics, and Working Class History, by David Roediger (New York: Verso, 1994).

Uprooting Racism: How White People Can Work for Racial Justice, rev. ed., by Paul Kivel (Branford, CT: New Society Publishers, 2002).

White Awareness: Handbook for Anti-Racism Training, by Judith H. Katz (Norman, OK: University of Oklahoma Press, 1978).

"White Folks": Seeing America through Black Eyes, by Lowell D. Thompson (Self-published, 1996).

"A White Perspective: Moving Up and Out of Racism," by Sandy Heidemann (*Newsline,* September 1994).

"White Privilege: Unpacking the Invisible Knapsack," by Peggy McIntosh (*Peace and Freedom,* July/August 1989).

White Privilege and Male Privilege: A Personal Account of Coming to See Correspondences through Work in Women's Studies, by Peggy McIntosh (Wellesley, MA: Wellesley College Center for Research on Women, 1988).

"White Racism," by Christine Sleeter (*Multicultural Education,* Spring 1994).

White Racism: The Basics, by Joe R. Feagin and Hernan Vera (New York: Routledge, 1995).

White Teacher, by Vivian Gussin Paley (Cambridge, MA: Harvard University Press, 1989).

Why Are All the Black Kids Sitting Together in the Cafeteria? rev. ed., by Beverly D. Tatum (New York: Basic Books, 2003).

Yours in Struggle: Three Feminist Perspectives on Anti-Semitism and Racism, by Elly Bulkin, Minnie Bruce Pratt, and Barbara Smith (Ithaca, NY: Firebrand Books, 1988).

Sexual Orientation

Stranger at the Gate: To Be Gay and Christian in America, by Mel White (New York: Simon and Schuster, 1994).

"Teachers and Parents Define Diversity in an Oregon Preschool Cooperative: Democracy at Work," by Jennifer Lakey (*Young Children,* May 1997).

"Working with Lesbian and Gay Parents and Their Children," by James W. Clay (*Young Children,* March 1990).

Work

Made by Human Hands: A Curriculum for Teaching Young Children about Work and Working People, by Jessie Wenning and Sheli Wortis (Cambridge, MA: The Multicultural Project for Communication and Education, 1985).

Resource Organizations

Claudia's Caravan: Multicultural Multilingual Materials, P. O. Box 1582, Alameda, CA 94501; telephone 510-521-7871. Supplier of books.

Council for Interracial Books for Children (CIBC). CIBC is no longer in existence. Its former address was 1841 Broadway, New York, NY 10023. Some local libraries carry CIBC publications and still have most of the issues of its *Bulletin.*

National Association for the Education of Young Children (NAEYC), 1834 Connecticut Avenue NW, Washington, DC 20009-5786; telephone 202-232-8777/800-424-2460. NAEYC has a publications catalog and holds an annual conference every year in November.

National Coalition of Education Activists (NCEA), 1420 Walnut St. #720, Philadelphia, PA 19102; telephone 215-735-2418; Web site: www.nceaonline.org. NCEA publishes a newsletter and holds a conference every summer.

New Society Publishers, P. O. Box 189, Gabriola Island, BC, Canada VOR 1X0; telephone 250-247-9737; Web site: www.newsociety.com. New Society Publishers is a not-for-profit, worker-controlled publishing house dedicated to promoting fundamental social change through nonviolent action.

Teaching for Change (formerly Network of Educators on the Americas), P. O. Box 73038, Washington, DC 20056; telephone 800-763-9131; Web site: www.teachingforchange.org. Teaching for Change offers an excellent selection of books and publishes some of its own resources. Call, write, or go to the Web site to order a free catalog.

TIDE (Teachers in Development Education), Birmingham, Millennium Point, GO4 Curzon Street, Birmingham B4 7XG; Web site: www.tidec.org. TIDE has produced several publications, including *Do It Justice! Resources and Activities for Introducing Education in Human Rights*; *Get the Picture! Developing Visual Literacy in the Infant (Preschool) Classroom*; *Hidden Messages: Activities for Exploring Bias*; *"Where It Really Matters": Developing Anti-Racist Education in Predominantly White Primary Schools*.

Suggested Books for Children

Alef Is One: A Hebrew Alphabet and Counting Book, by Katherine Janus Kahn (Rockville, MD: Kar-Ben Copies, 1989). Hebrew letters introduce the concept of counting, from one lion to four hundred parrots.

All the Colors We Are/Todos los Colores de Nuestra Piel: The Story of How We Get Our Skin Color/La Historia de por que Tenemos Diferentes Colores de Piel, by Katie Kissinger (St. Paul: Redleaf Press, 1994). With beautiful photographs and simple text, this book carefully and clearly explains how we get our skin color. Several relevant activities are included to go with the book.

Amazing Grace, by Mary Hoffman (New York: Dial Books, 1991). A young African American girl wants to be Peter Pan in the school play. A classmate tells her she can't play that role because Peter Pan isn't black. Grace's family provides the support she needs to be what she wants to be. PROBLEM: The illustrations include two stereotypical images. In the first, Grace is dressed in a stereotypical multifeathered Native American headdress playing Hiawatha. In the second, Grace is dressed as a pirate with a wooden leg and an eye patch. This is offensive to people with substitute limbs or eye patches; it perpetuates the idea that these physical characteristics are always associated with pirates.

Amelia's Road, by Linda Jacobs Altman (New York: Lee & Low Books, 1993). Tired of moving around so much with her migrant farm-worker family, Amelia dreams of a stable home.

Angel Child, Dragon Child, by Michele Maria Surat (New York: Scholastic, 1989). A young girl experiences discrimination because of her Vietnamese clothing and accent. Her classmate confronts and changes his prejudice toward her and in the end helps her with a problem. PROBLEM: When Raymond, the teaser, is shocked that Ut "didn't use funny words" to speak to him, Ut responds proudly: "I say English." This leaves the message that languages other than English sound "funny" rather than simply different and that pride comes with learning English and not from both learning English and maintaining one's first language.

Anna Banana and Me, by Lenore Blegvad (New York: Aladdin Books, 1987). Anna Banana's fearlessness inspires a playmate to face his fears.

Asha's Mums, by Rosamund Elwin and Michele Paulse (Toronto: Women's Press, 1990). The teacher tells Asha, "You can't have two mums." The story includes a wonderful class discussion and debate about whether or not, and why and why not, you can or cannot have two mums.

Ashok by Any Other Name, by Sandra S. Yamate (Chicago: Polychrome Publishing, 1992). This is a story of Ashok, an Indian American boy who wishes he had a less ethnic, more "American" name. His experiments with new names create a variety of mishaps until he finally discovers just the right name for himself.

Babushka Baba Yaga, by Patricia Polacco (New York: Philomel Books, 1993). This is a story about stereotyping. The villagers are afraid of her, so the legendary Baba Yaga disguises herself as an old woman in order to know the joys of being a grandmother. Fear of discovery forces her back into the forest. A child loses a grandmother, and the village babushkas lose a friend. In the end they discover how wonderful the Baba Yaga is, and she is welcomed back to the village.

Bein' with You This Way, by W. Nikola-Lisa (New York: Lee & Low Books, 1995). On a beautiful day, a little girl visits the park and rounds up a group of her friends. As they play they celebrate their diversity—straight hair, curly hair; light skin, dark skin—with wonderful rhyming verse.

Be Good to Eddie Lee, by Virginia Fleming (New York: Philomel Books, 1993). This is a story about friendship and diverse physical and mental abilities.

Belinda's Bouquet, by Lesléa Newman (Boston: Alyson Wonderland, 1991). A child, teased about being fat, is aided by a friend who has two moms.

Best Friends, by Miriam Cohen (New York: Simon and Schuster Children's, 1971). Young friends fight and make up.

Big Al, by Andrew Clements (New York: Scholastic, 1991). Big Al is a nice fish, but he is big and scary-looking and has no friends. One day Big Al proves what a good friend he could be. PROBLEM: Someone who is "different" (Big Al) has to prove himself by being a super-friend rather than being accepted because differences are okay.

Bird Talk, by Lenore Keeshig-Tobias (Toronto: Sister Vision: Black Women and Women of Colour Press, 1991). Story of a Native child who hears at school, "If you're Indian why don't you come from India?" and "Where's your feathers then?'" She is strengthened by her mother's support, which includes stories of Mishomis and the real facts about Christopher Columbus. Order from Oyate, 2702 Mathews Street, Berkeley, CA 94702; telephone 510-848-6700; Web site: www.oyate.org.

Black Like Kyra, White Like Me, by Judith Vigna (Morton Grove, IL: Albert Whitman & Co., 1992). A black family moves into an all-white neighborhood. Christy, who is white, faces peer pressure to reject her friend. Both she and her family confront the prejudice and maintain their friendship with Kyra's family even though they are rejected by white friends. This book is one of the few available stories dealing directly with racism. PROBLEM: According to the story, Kyra's family wants to move because of all the crime in their present neighborhood. I believe that these references would be better taken out. There are many reasons why a black family would want to move—the need for a larger home, for example. The inclusion of these negative references to a "bad neighborhood" perpetuates a stereotype of high crime in black neighborhoods.

Boundless Grace, by Mary Hoffman (New York: Dial Books, 1995). Grace has negative feelings about the composition of her family—

her mother and father are separated. She goes to visit her father in Africa and deals with feelings of jealousy. Sequel to *Amazing Grace.*

The Bracelet, by Yoshiko Uchida (New York: Philomel Books, 1993). The United States is at war with Japan, and Emi and her family are being sent to a prison camp because they are Japanese Americans. They haven't done anything wrong but are being treated like the enemy just because they look like the enemy. Emi's best friend comes to say good-bye and brings her a bracelet so she will remember their friendship.

Bread, Bread, Bread, by Ann Morris (New York: Lothrop, 1989). Excellent photographs illustrating a relevant cross-cultural theme.

Building an Igloo, by Ulli Steltzer (New York: Henry Holt, 1995). Tookillkee Kiguktak does not live in an igloo; like most Inuit of today he lives in a house of wood. But when Tookillkee was a little child he lived in an igloo, and when he was a boy he learned how to build one. When he goes hunting far away for a musk ox or a polar bear, he builds an igloo for shelter.

The Carousel, by Liz Rosenberg (New York: Harcourt Brace, 1995). Two sisters find that the horses of a broken carousel have come alive in the rain. The story is a fantasy of courage and adventure that weaves in the sisters' memories of their mother, who "had been someone who could fix anything, from leaky faucets to broken porch lights and banisters, washing machines, and more." The sisters have acquired their mother's skills and use what she has taught them to fix the broken carousel.

Char Siu Bao Boy, by Sandra S. Yamate (Chicago: Polychrome Publishing, 1991). Charlie is a Chinese American boy who likes to eat char siu bao (barbecued pork buns) for lunch. His friends find his eating preferences odd, and Charlie succumbs to peer pressure. He tries to eat "normal" food, only to find he is not happy. Eventually, Charlie finds a way to overcome his classmates' aversion to his ethnic food as they learn to try new foods before they decide that they dislike them.

Chicken Sunday, Patricia Polacco (New York: Philomel Books, 1992). This is the story of a white child's close relationship with a black family. There is an elderly Jewish man who has a hat store. The children want to get a special Easter hat for grandmother, but the store owner, who is often teased by neighborhood children, thinks that they are up to no good.

Children Just Like Me: A Unique Celebration of Children around the World, by Barnabus Kindersley et al. (New York: DK Publishing,

1995). This book has wonderful photographs and family stories of children from all over the globe. Most of the children dress in daily wear and talk about daily activities. PROBLEM: The families represented lack diversity: they all have two heterosexual parents.

Children's Home, by Hoonie Feltham and Margaret Robson (London: A & C Black, 1986). A child lives in institutional care.

Clive Eats Alligators, by Alison Lester (Boston: Houghton Mifflin, 1991). Seven children are each pictured doing different daily routines in their own way.

Colors around Me, by Vivian Church (Chicago: African American Images, 1993). To celebrate the diversity of color of black people, children with different tones of brown, black, and beige are compared to positive pleasing things in their environment.

Come Sit by Me, by Margaret Merrifield (Buffalo: Stoddart Kids, 1998). Friends deal with AIDS.

Cornrows, by Camille Yarbrough (New York: Putnam, 1997). Covers African American hairstyling.

A Country Far Away, by Nigel Gray (New York: Orchard Books, 1989). Two children in very different places tell similar stories about their day. Bilingual Hindi and English.

Daddy and Me, by Jeanne Moutoussamy-Ashe (New York: Knopf, 1993). The relationship between Arthur Ashe and his daughter, Camera, thrived even in the face of AIDS.

Daddy's Roommate, by Michael Willhoite (Los Angeles: Alyson Publications, 1990). A boy has two fathers.

The Day of Ahmed's Secret, by Florence Parry Heide and Judith Heide Gilliland (New York: Mulberry, 1995). Amid daily life in an Arab city, Ahmed waits to tell his family his secret: he has learned to write his name.

Dulcie Dando, Soccer Star, by Sue Stops (New York: Henry Holt, 1992). Dulcie is a wonderful soccer player, but the boys don't want her on the team. In the end the team needs Dulcie, who scores the winning goal. PROBLEM: Girls should be welcome on the soccer team even if they don't score the winning goal.

Eating Fractions, by Bruce McMillan (New York: Scholastic, 1992). Two close friends, one white and one black, are pictured throughout the illustrations of food and fractions.

Fat Fat Rose Marie, by Lisa Passen (New York: Henry Holt, 1991). Rose Marie is teased because of her size. Her friend Claire is coaxed away to join with the teasers. Claire eventually stands up for her friend, risking the disapproval of the teasers. The story illustrates how children encounter difficulties like these but can still take positive action. PROBLEM: The title is problematic and in one class became a chant before children understood the story. One suggestion is to brainstorm, with children, a new title. Some also object to Claire's solution, which is to mush her ice cream in the face of the teaser. Having children discuss their opinions about Claire's solution and what else she might do and what they could do in a similar situation helps to deal with this problem.

Finding the Green Stone, by Alice Walker (New York: Harcourt Brace, 1997). Everyone in Johnny's town has a green stone that reflects their conscience; when Johnny loses his, he begins to behave badly. His community helps him to search for his stone, and when he finds it, he regains his integrity and his love for others.

Finger Foods, Chris Despande, photographs by Prodeepta Das (London: A & C Black, 1988). Cross-cultural picnic of foods awaits children, who can eat with their fingers.

Flossie and the Fox, by Patricia C. McKissack (New York: Dial Books, 1986). A wily fox notorious for stealing eggs meets his match when he encounters a bold little girl in the woods who insists upon proof that he is a fox before she will be frightened. The book is written in Black English.

Fly Away Home, by Eve Bunting (Boston: Houghton Mifflin, 1993). A homeless boy, Andrew, lives in an airport with his father, moving from terminal to terminal and trying not to be noticed. Andrew's father works as a janitor on weekends. He is searching for an apartment but has been unable to find one he can afford. PROBLEM: Two other homeless men, portrayed as loud drunks, and a woman with a cart "full of stuff" and a "long, dirty coat" are all caught by security because they are noticeable. Why was it necessary to include these stereotypes in the story? They imply that homelessness is an individual problem and can be taken care of by being careful not to get caught and working hard to get one's life back together, rather than a societal problem that must be addressed by creating affordable housing and jobs for everyone. The story also perpetuates a stereotype about Latinos not valuing education as much as white people do. For Andrew's father it is "important" that Andrew start school in the fall. But in a sentence that could easily have been left out of the book, it is explained that for Mrs. Medina and her son Denny, who is seven, it is not so important and Denny can wait for a while.

Follow the Drinking Gourd, by Jeanette Winter (New York: Dragonfly Books, 1992). By following the directions in a song, "The Drinking Gourd," runaway slaves journey north along the Underground Railroad to freedom in Canada.

A Forever Family, by Roslyn Banish (New York: HarperCollins, 1992). This story covers adoption.

Friday Night Is Papa Night, by Emily A. McCully (New York: Puffin Books, 1989). A father who works a distance from home comes home every Friday night.

Friends from the Other Side/Amigos del otro lado, by Gloria Anzaldúa (San Francisco: Children's Book Press, 1995). Joaquin, who has crossed the Rio Grande River into Texas with his mother in search of a better life, is protected by Prietita, a brave Mexican American girl. Prietita defends Joaquin from the neighborhood kids, who taunt him with shouts of "mojado," or "wetback." She finds a way to protect Joaquin and his mother from the Border Patrol.

Go Team! by Michi Fujimoto (New York: Putnam, 1996). Why is it that the boys keep losing to the girls at tug-of-war? Isn't it a "manly" rope game, and not like the silly jumping rope games that girls play? The boys learn that the girls' valuable secret of working together is the best strategy of all, and jumping rope is for both boys and girls.

Good Morning Franny, Good Night Franny, by Emily Hearn (Toronto: The Women's Press, 1984). Franny is an active young girl in a wheelchair who forms a friendship with Ting. PROBLEM: The illustrations of Ting and her mother are disappointing. Their eyes are portrayed as slits rather than full eyes.

Haitian Days: Ti Djo Remembers, by Marcus Plaisimond (Littleton, MA: Sundance Publishers, 1993). Ti Djo remembers the things he used to do in Haiti. The illustrations are beautiful paintings by various Haitian artists, and the text is trilingual in English, French, and Creole.

Halmoni and the Picnic, by Sook Nyul Choi (Boston: Houghton Mifflin, 1993). Yunmi's grandmother has just moved to New York City from Korea, and she's finding it difficult to feel comfortable. The customs are so different, and she is too shy to speak English. When her grandmother is invited to join her third-grade class picnic, Yunmi worries that her classmates will make fun of her grandmother's traditional dress and Korean food. Instead it is a wonderful experience, and Yunmi's grandmother feels much more comfortable after the picnic.

Hats Off to Hair! by Virginia Kroll (Watertown, MA: Charlesbridge, 1995). Celebrates the many different ways we wear our hair—long, short, curly, knotted, twisted, braided, beaded, and so on.

He Bear She Bear, by Stan Berenstain and Jan Berenstain (New York: Random House, 1974). Two bears, a brother and sister, speculate on all the things they could grow up to be.

Here Comes Kate! by Judy Carlson (Chatham, NJ: Raintree Steck-Vaughn Publishers, 1989). Kate just loves to go fast in her wheel-chair but often goes too fast and causes a variety of difficulties for others. She becomes interested in wheelchair races that she sees on TV.

I Can't Sleep! by Michi Fujimoto (New York: Putnam, 1996). During a slumber party the kids find that they can't get to sleep without their regular bedtime routines. Each has different habits. With a little in-genuity and a lot of cooperation, they manage to do what each of them needs to fall asleep.

I Hate My Name! by Eva Grant (Milwaukee: Raintree Steck-Vaughn, 1980). After starting school, a girl with an unusual first name weighs the pains of being ridiculed and feeling different against the pleasures of having a unique identity and learning to appreciate others' names.

I'm Not Frightened of Ghosts, by Juliet Snape and Charles Snape (Upper Saddle River, NJ: Prentice Hall Books for Young Readers, 1987). A young girl, alone but unafraid, enters a big old house with ghosts.

I'm the Big Sister Now, by Michelle Emmert (Morton Grove, IL: Albert Whitman, 1989). Michelle's older sister was born with cerebral palsy. Michelle tells her sister's story.

It Takes a Village, by Jane Cowen-Fletcher (New York: Scholastic, 1994). Mother goes to market with two children, knowing other people will help look out for them.

Jambo Means Hello: Swahili Alphabet Book, by Muriel Feelings and Tom Feelings (New York: Puffin Books, 1985). From A to Z, Swahili words recreate the traditions of East African village life. Keep in mind balancing this with urban images of Africa as well.

Jennifer Has Two Daddies, by Priscilla Galloway (Toronto: The Women's Press, 1983). Jennifer's parents are divorced. One week she lives with Mummy and Michael and the next week with her daddy.

Jeremy's Dreidel, by Ellie Gellman (Rockville, MD: Kar-Ben Copies, 1992). This story is about celebrations and diverse physical abilities, especially blindness.

Less than Half, More than Whole, by Kathleen Lacapa and Michael Lacapa (Flagstaff, AZ: Northland Publishing, 1994). Native American identity is explored.

Lights on the River, by Jane Resh Thomas (New York: Hyperion Books for Children, 1994). A story of migrant farmworkers from Mexico working on U.S. farms. The story illustrates the power of family as well as the difficult life and mistreatment farmworkers face. A story for young children of farmworkers organizing against some of the mistreatment would be a helpful companion.

The Little Weaver of Thai-Yen Village, by Tran-Khanh-Tuyet (San Francisco: Children's Book Press, 1987). This story is about a young Vietnamese girl. She lives in a village that helps another that has been bombed. Then her village gets bombed too. The young girl's parents are killed. She is wounded and taken to the United States and continues to help Vietnam by weaving and sending blankets.

Living in Two Worlds, by Maxine B. Rosenberg (New York: Lothrop, Lee & Shepard Books, 1986). Covers biracial families, race, and racism.

The Lorax, by Dr. Seuss (New York: Random House, 1971). This is a good book for reconsidering cooperative strategies. Discussion with children could have them examine alternative ways the Lorax could have fought the pollution caused by the Once-ler as he manufactures Thneeds. The Lorax tries to stop the pollution by himself. Perhaps, instead of sending away Bar-ba-loots, the Swomee-Swans, and the Humming-Fish, he could have helped bring them all together to organize against the pollution.

Louise Builds a House, by Louise Pfanner (New York: Orchard Books, 1989). A fanciful girl builds a house, gives it to her sister, and goes on to build a boat.

Margaret and Margarita, by Lynn Reiser (New York: Mulberry Books, 1996). This bilingual book is about two girls who meet in the park. One speaks Spanish, and the other speaks English. Each child speaks to the other in her own language, and each is saying the same thing.

Marshmallows, Monsters, and Mice, by Wendy Hartmann (Cape Town, South Africa: Songololo Books, 1990). A young girl takes control of her nightmares.

Matthew and Tilly, by Rebecca J. Jones (New York: Puffin Books, 1995). Close friends have a disagreement and resolve their conflict.

Max, by Rachel Isadora (New York: Aladdin, 1984). A boy gets into ballet dancing.

Moja Means One: Swahili Counting Book, by Muriel Feelings (New York: Puffin Books, 1976). Counting book in Swahili pictures East African village life. Keep in mind balancing this with urban images of Africa as well.

Mrs. Katz and Tush, by Patricia Polacco (New York: Bantam Little Rooster, 1992). A young African American boy befriends an elderly Jewish woman.

My Dad Takes Care of Me, by Patricia Quinlan (Toronto: Annick Press, 1987). Luke's father is unemployed, but Luke tells everyone he's a pilot. The story shows some of the changes the family has had to make because of unemployment.

My Grandma Has Black Hair, by Mary Hoffman (New York: Dial Books for Young Readers, 1988). This book contrasts "my grandma" with all of the typical stereotypes.

My Grandson Lew, by Charlotte Zolotow (New York: HarperCollins Children's Books, 2004). Lewis remembers lots of wonderful things about his grandfather, who has died.

My Mom Can't Read, by Muriel Stanek (Morton Grove, IL: Albert Whitman, 1986). A young girl learning to read at school discovers that her mom can't read.

My Mother the Mail Carrier/Mi Mama la Cartera, by Inez Maury (New York: The Feminist Press, 1976). A five-year-old describes the loving and close relationship she has with her mother, a mail carrier, and also relates some aspects of her mother's job.

The Nutmeg Princess, by Richardo Keens-Douglas (Toronto: Annick Press, 1992). This fantasy story is set in Grenada. Two children manage to see the Nutmeg Princess, seen by no one else except Petite Mama, because of their unselfishness and friendship.

Old Hat, New Hat, by Stan Berenstain and Jan Berenstain (New York: Random House, 1997). After trying exciting new hats, Brother Bear finds that the old hat turns out to be just right.

Oliver Button Is a Sissy, by Tomie dePaola (New York: Harcourt Brace Jovanovich, 1979). Oliver is teased for doing ballet, but the taunts don't stop him from doing what he likes best. In the end the teasers decide he's a star.

On the Go, by Ann Morris (New York: Lothrop, Lee & Shepard Books, 1990). Part of Ann Morris's series of books on cross-cultural themes with wonderful photographs from all over the world. This book chronicles the ways we transport people and things.

Our Teacher's in a Wheelchair, by Mary Ellen Powers (Morton Grove, IL: Albert Whitman & Company, 1986). Brian Hanson teaches in a child care center. The book talks about what he can do with his wheelchair. It also talks about children's fears about "catching it."

The Owl and the Woodpecker, by Brian Wildsmith (New York: Oxford University Press, 1992). The woodpecker pecks and disturbs the owl, who sleeps during the day. The other animals get involved in finding a way to resolve their dispute.

The Paper Bag Princess, by Robert Munsch (Toronto: Annick Press, 1986). Elizabeth, a young princess, is about to marry Prince Ronald. Unfortunately, a dragon burned all her clothes and carried off Prince Ronald. Dressed only in a paper bag, Elizabeth follows and outsmarts the dragon and releases Prince Ronald. Elizabeth then rejects the ungrateful prince, who is more concerned with the fact that she smells like ashes and is dressed in a dirty paper bag than with her bravery or his own freedom.

Paul and Sebastian, by René Escudie (Brooklyn: Kane-Miller Books, 1994). Paul, who lives in a trailer, and Sebastian, who lives in an apartment, are discouraged from playing with each other by their mothers, who each feel disdainful of the other's living situation. The boys discover that even though their homes are so different, they can be friends.

Pearl Moscowitz's Last Stand, by Arthur A. Levine (New York: Tambourine Books, 1993). Pearl Moscowitz, an elderly Jewish woman living in a diverse urban neighborhood, supported by her neighbors, takes a stand when the city government tries to chop down the last gingko tree on the street.

The People Who Hugged the Trees: An Environmental Folk Tale, by Deborah Lee Rose (Lanham, MD: Roberts Rinehart, 2001). A young girl leads her community to stand up against the soldiers of the Maharajah to prevent them from cutting down the trees that protect the village from sandstorms.

Prietita and the Ghost Woman/Prietita y la llorona, by Gloria Anzaldúa (San Francisco: Children's Book Press, 1996). Prietita, a young Mexican American girl, goes in search of an herb to cure her mother. She becomes lost and is aided by a legendary ghost woman. Prietita discovers that the ghost woman is not what people expect but rather a compassionate woman who helps her on her path.

Pueblo Story Teller, by Diane Hoyt-Goldsmith (New York: Holiday House, 1991). This book celebrates present-day pottery making, bread baking, storytelling, drum making, and Buffalo Dance.

Purnima's Parrot, by Feroza Mathieson (London: Magi Publications, 1988). Purnima wishes her parrot could talk instead of just saying things like "Craark." She discovers it can talk, but in a language she can't understand.

Race You, Franny, by Emily Hearn (Toronto: Women's Educational Press, 1986). Franny, an active young girl, is in a wheelchair.

The Rag Coat, by Lauren Mills (Boston: Little, Brown, 1991). Minna, who lives in Appalachia, wants to go to school. First she needs a winter coat. The Quilting Mothers offer to make her a coat from scraps of quilting material. Minna proudly wears the new coat to school but gets teased for her rag coat.

Ragsale, by Artie Ann Bates (Boston: Houghton Mifflin, 1995). Jessann and her family spend Saturday going to the rag sales of their Appalachian town.

The Rainbow Fish, by Marcus Pfister (New York: North-South Books, 1996). The most beautiful fish in the ocean discovers that the value of sharing and friendship is far greater than being beautiful without friends.

Rainbow Fish to the Rescue, by Marcus Pfister (New York: North-South Books, 1996). A striped fish wants to join a group of fish but is left out. A shark enters the reef, and all the fish make it to safety except for the striped one. Rainbow Fish organizes the other fish to help the striped fish.

The Rajah's Rice: A Mathematical Folktale from India, by David Barry (New York: W. H. Freeman, 1994). On rent collection day, villagers must turn over to the Rajah most of the rice they have grown. Many of the villagers will go hungry. When the Rajah's elephants get sick, Chandra is the only one who can make them well. To make them well, she demands in exchange what appears to be a very simple mathematical formula of rice for the village. The Rajah agrees, only to discover that the formula multiplies into so much rice that he is unable to pay it. In the end he must agree to give the people of the village the land that they farm and to take only as much rice as he really needs for himself.

The Red Comb, by Fernando Pico (Moraga, CA: BridgeWater Books, 1996). Set in nineteenth-century Puerto Rico, two women, one old and one young, plot to save a runaway slave.

The River that Gave Gifts: An Afro-American Story, by Margo Humphrey (San Francisco: Children's Book Press, 1995). In this African American story, three sisters create beautiful presents for their grandmother before she loses her eyesight. It shows that the best presents are often made with love, not bought with money.

Sachiko Means Happiness, by Kimiko Sakai (San Francisco: Children's Book Press, 1994). The story is about a young Japanese girl and her relationship with her grandmother, who has Alzheimer's disease. PROBLEM: This is a wonderful story, but it must be balanced with many other stories that show elderly people leading active lives.

Sam Johnson and the Blue Ribbon Quilt, by Lisa Campbell Ernst (New York: Mulberry Books, 1992). Sam discovers that he enjoys sewing but meets with ridicule when he asks his wife if he can join her quilting club. Sam forms a men's quilting group. In the end both groups have to cooperate to make a quilt.

Sami and the Time of the Troubles, by Florence Parry Heide and Judith Heide Gilliland (Boston: Clarion Books, 1992). A ten-year-old Lebanese boy goes to school, helps with chores, plays with friends, and lives with his family in a basement shelter when bombings occur and fighting begins on his street. The book gives a positive sense of something that can be done in this situation: the children have a demonstration against war.

Seeing in Special Ways, by Thomas Bergman (Milwaukee: Gareth Stevens Children's Books, 1989). Interviews with children reveal attitudes about blindness.

Sitti's Secrets, by Naomi Shihab Nye (New York: Four Winds Press, 1997). A young girl describes a visit to see her grandmother in a Palestinian village in the West Bank.

The Sneetches and Other Stories, by Dr. Seuss (New York: Random House, 1966). Classic book about prejudice based on physical characteristics: "The Star-Belly Sneetches had bellies with stars. The Plain-Belly Sneetches had none upon thars. . . . The Star-Belly Sneetches would brag, 'We're the best kind of Sneetch on the beaches. . . . We'll have nothing to do with the Plain-Belly sort!'"

Somewhere in Africa, by Ingrid Mennen and Niki Daly (New York: Dutton Children's Books, 1992). Challenging stereotypes about Africa, the story is about Ashraf, who lives in an African city and has only seen "wild and untamed animals in a book borrowed from the city library."

Stellaluna, by Janell Cannon (New York: Harcourt Brace, 1993). A bat separated from her mother joins a family of birds. As a bat, according to the birds, the bat hangs upside down, and so on. The bat asks, "How can we be so different and feel so much alike?"

The Streets Are Free, by Monika Doppert (Toronto: Annick Press, 1995). Children organize to get a playground.

Swimmy, by Leo Lionni (New York: Alfred A. Knopf, 1963). All the little fish get together to protect themselves from the big fish.

T Is for "Terrific," by Mahji Hall (Seattle: Open Hand Publishing, 1989). Bilingual alphabet book in English and Spanish.

Talk to Me, by Sue Brearley (London: A & C Black, 1996). Not everyone starts to speak at the same age, in the same way. Some children have problems with speaking clearly. Some can't speak at all and must find a different way of talking. This book covers many of the issues associated with talking: Deafness, sign language, physical differences that inhibit speech, speech therapists, using symbol language, learning slowly, hard work learning to speak, getting frustrated and mixing up words, needing others to pay attention and listen, lip-reading, and patience.

Tap-Tap, by Karen Lynn Williams (Boston: Clarion Books, 1996). Market day in a village in Haiti is the focus. *Tap-taps* are colorful buses that serve as transportation through much of Haiti.

Teammates, by Peter Golenbock (New York: Harcourt Brace, 1990). This is the story of the racial prejudice experienced by Jackie Robinson when he joined the Brooklyn Dodgers and how white teammate Pee Wee Reese challenged some of the racism.

This Is Our House, by Michael Rosen (Cambridge, MA: Candlewick Press, 1996). George won't let any of the other children into his cardboard box house until he finds out how it feels to be excluded.

Through My Window, by Tony Bradman and Eileen Browne (Morristown, NJ: Silver Burdett, 1986). Jo is ill and must stay indoors while Dad looks after her and Mum goes to work. Jo's mother is black, and her father is white. The street scenes that Jo sees from her window are racially and culturally diverse, and other roles are nontraditional.

True or False? by Patricia Ruben (New York: J. B. Lippincott, 1978). Photographs are paired with true-or-false questions.

Wait and See, by Tony Bradman and Eileen Browne (New York: Oxford University Press, 1988). Jo's dad is white, and her mom is black. Jo and her mom go out shopping while her dad stays home and prepares lunch. As they do their errands, they talk to neighbors and shopkeepers of diverse races, cultures, and ages.

We Can Do It! by Laura Dwight (Yardley, PA: Checkerboard Press, 1992). Photo essay covers several children with a range of physical challenges.

Welcoming Babies, by Margy Burns Knight (Gardiner, ME: Tilbury House, 1998). This book celebrates the diversity of ways that babies are welcomed.

What Is Beautiful? by Maryjean Watson Avery and David M. Avery (Berkeley: Tricycle Press, 1995). This book encourages children to recognize different forms of beauty in various individuals and to see what is beautiful about themselves.

Who Belongs Here? An American Story, by Margy Burns Knight (Gardiner, ME: Tilbury House Publishers, 1996). Nary is a young boy who fled with his grandmother from the brutality of Pol Pot and the Khmer Rouge in Cambodia. Now in the United States, Nary is teased by his classmates. He tells the teacher of his difficulties, and together they plan a lesson that will help other children to understand Nary better. There are parallel anecdotes relating the experiences of other refugees. The format of the book is a little complicated but can be adapted. It is also an excellent book to use with staff as a catalyst for discussion about refugees to the United States and related issues.

Who's in a Family? by Robert Skutch (Berkeley: Tricycle Press, 1998). Families can be made up in many different ways. Gay and lesbian families are included.

Willie's Not the Hugging Kind, by Joyce Durham Barrett (New York: HarperCollins, 1991). This book explores alternative gender roles.

William's Doll, by Charlotte Zolotow (New York, HarperCollins, 1971). A young boy who loves model trains and basketball still wants a doll to play with. The book portrays his grandmother in a positive, nonstereotypical way as the person most sensitive to William's desire for a doll.

Working Cotton, by Sherley Anne Williams (New York: Harcourt Brace, 1997). A young black girl relates the daily events of her family's migrant life in the cotton fields of central California.

You Be Me, I'll Be You, by Pili Mandelbaum (Brooklyn: Kane/Miller Book Publishers, 1990). An interracial child says, "But daddy, I don't like the color of my face, or of my hands. . . . I want to be like you." "How silly. . . . I would do anything not to have this pale face of mine." The discussion continues, and they talk about mixing paints and then coffee and milk to match their skin tones. Eventually brown-skinned daughter and white-skinned father experiment to see what it would be like to have the other's skin color and hairstyles.

Index

comparisons, pitfalls of, 46

competition, 42–43

confident identity, 2

conflict, 19, 22, 81, 107–108, 110–111

conformism, 40, 44

confrontation guidelines, 108

consumerism, 41, 44

conversational styles, 80–81

cooperation, 41–43

copyright dates, 101

critical thinking, 15, 17–18

cultural groups
  awareness of differences in, 1–3, 18–19
  expressions of friendship, 35
  and language bias, 61
  visual images of, 63–64, 91

cultural values, in stereotypical story lines, 58–60

culture, defined, 53

curriculum, hidden, 20

curriculum themes, 70

D

defensiveness, bias and, 4, 15–16, 54, 78–80

DeRosa, Patti, 13

developmental disabilities, 45

differences
  awareness of, 1–2, 8–9, 85–86
  in conversational styles, 80–81
  in experience of bias, 10–11
  guiding awareness about, 3–4, 108
  learning about, checklist for, 83
  in personal style, 19
  values related to, 9–10

disabilities. *See* physical abilities and characteristics

disagreements, bias and, 32, 81

discrimination, 4, 8–9, 33, 107. *See also* biases

discussion questions
  ageism, 25–26
  anti-bias approach, 5, 7, 14, 20–21

classism, 42–44

communication styles and participation, 19–20

cultural groups, 2–3

design of, 1

differences, 3–4, 9–10

experience of bias, 10–11

gender bias, 31–32

internalized messages, 4

perpetuation of biases, unintentional, 16

physical abilities and characteristics, 50–51

race and ethnicity, 64–67

self-identity, 2–3

sexual orientation, 36–37

standing up against injustice, 5

understanding bias, 17–18

discussions
  dynamic style of, 80–81
  formats for, 76–77
  leading difficult, 78–79
  participation in, 82–83
  patterns of bias in, 19
  tips for tough spots, 79–82

diversity
  absence of, 12
  awareness of, 2–3
  checklists for, 85–86, 94–96
  in experience of bias, 10–11
  in families, scenarios, 37

dramatic play checklist, 94

drug users, stereotypes about, 15

E

economic class, 19, 39–44, 123

educational conditions for anti-bias approach, 2

elderly people, 23–26, 90–91

Elders, Jocelyn, 37

equality, struggles for, 29

ethnic diversity, absence of, 12–13

ethnic groups, bias and, 61, 63–64, 91

ethnicity, 19, 53

ethnocentrism, 19, 53–54

Eurocentrism, 53

F

facilitator guidelines, 19, 75–82
familiarity and bias, 13
families, dysfunctional, 42
family composition, visual images
    of, 88–89
fantasy, 40, 43
feelings, gender bias and expression
    of, 31
female images, 29
femininity, sexism and definitions of,
    27
field trips, strategies for, 71–72
Filipino American men, 57
fish bowl, 77
framework for anti-bias approach, 7
friendships, cultural expressions of,
    35–36

G

gay men, 33, 35
gender bias, 27–32
gender identity, 30
grandparents, 25
group discussion formats, 76–77
growth, assumptions about, 82
guests, classroom strategies for, 72

H

handicap, as rejected term, 48
heroes, stereotypical, 21, 60, 99
heterosexism, 33–38
heterosexuality, 33, 36
history, in stereotypical story lines,
    59–60
holidays and heterosexism, 37
homeless people, stereotypes about,
    9
homophobia, 33–34, 36
homosexuality, 33–35

I

identity, construction of, 2, 64
illustrators of children's books, 100

injustices, standing up against, 4–5
institutional discrimination, 33, 45,
    54
integration of schools, 17
intentions, good, and negative im-
    pact, 15
interactions, diversity in, 3, 13
internalized oppression, 2, 10, 12
interruptions, gender bias and, 31
interventions in discrimination, 4–5,
    84, 107–110

J

Japanese American men, 57

K

knowledgeable identity, 2

L

language, 95, 107
language, stereotypical
    age and, 24–25
    gender and, 29–32, 100
    physical abilities and characteris-
        tics, 48–50
    race and ethnicity and, 58–59,
        61–63, 100
    sexual orientation and, 34–35
Latinos/Latinas, 55, 57
learning environment assessment,
    85
lesbians, 33, 35
lifestyle depictions, evaluation of,
    98–99
The Lion King (movie), 21
listening, defined, 80
literacy skills, 22
loaded terms, 61–63, 100
log of comments, 77

M

manual labor, 39, 41
masculinity, sexism and definitions
    of, 27

Other Resources from Redleaf Press

THAT'S NOT FAIR! A TEACHER'S GUIDE TO ACTIVISM WITH YOUNG CHILDREN

by Ann Pelo and Fran Davidson

Real-life stories of activist children, combined with teachers' experiences and reflections, create a complete guide to childhood activism.

BIG AS LIFE: THE EVERYDAY INCLUSIVE CURRICULUM, VOLUMES 1 & 2

by Stacey York

From the author of *Roots and Wings*, these two theme-based curriculum books offer sixteen information-packed units on favorite topics such as family, feelings, and animals. Each unit has suggested materials, learning area setup ideas, book lists, and loads of activities in all development areas. An essential resource for new and experienced teachers!

NOBODY ELSE LIKE ME: ACTIVITIES TO CELEBRATE DIVERSITY

by Sally Moomaw

A musical celebration of the diversity of children, *Nobody Else Like Me* gives teachers and children a joyful way to begin talking about our differences.

LESSONS FROM TURTLE ISLAND: NATIVE CURRICULUM IN EARLY CHILDHOOD CLASSROOMS

by Guy W. Jones and Sally Moomaw

This is the first complete guide to exploring Native American issues with children. Includes five cross-cultural themes—Children, Home, Families, Community, and the Environment.

ROOTS AND WINGS: AFFIRMING CULTURE IN EARLY CHILDHOOD PROGRAMS, REVISED EDITION

by Stacey York

Completely updated, this new edition retains the best of the original while presenting current anti-bias and culturally relevant issues in educating young children in a clear and organized way.

PLAY LADY/LA SEÑORA JUGUETONA

by Eric Hoffman
illustrated by Suzanne Tornquist

The moving story about how the kids in the neighborhood help their Play Lady after she's the victim of a hate crime. This wonderful children's book also includes activity and teaching ideas for caregivers and is bilingual in English and Spanish.

NO FAIR TO TIGERS/NO ES JUSTO PARA LOS TIGRES

by Eric Hoffman
illustrated by Janice Lee Porter

This colorful children's book is a story about Mandy, a girl with a disability, and how her stuffed tiger shows how they ask for fair treatment and solutions to the problems they encounter. Includes activity and teaching ideas for caregivers. Bilingual English/Spanish.

800-423-8309
www.redleafpress.org